The Second Newman Report:
National Policy and Higher Education

The MIT Press
Cambridge, Massachusetts, and London, England

The Second Newman Report:
National Policy and Higher Education

Report of a Special Task Force to the
Secretary of Health, Education, and Welfare

, P 2I · ⬤

This book was set in Linotype Baskerville
printed on Nashoba blue white antique
and bound in linen finish #144
by The Colonial Press Inc.
in the United States of America.

Library of Congress catalog card number: 73–21475
ISBN 0–262–08071–0 (hardcover)
ISBN 0–262–58027–6 (paperback)

Contents

Foreword

In March 1971, HEW published *Report on Higher Education,* a study by a nongovernmental task force chaired by Frank Newman of Stanford University. The purpose of this study was to assess, in general terms, how well higher education was meeting the needs of society in the 1970s. The *Report* did not propose solutions, but rather characterized problems from the perspective, not of the federal government nor of educational institutions, but of an independent group, privately financed and acting in the public interest.

Following the release of the *Report,* we asked Frank Newman to take on a second and more difficult assignment—to recommend some specific ways in which the federal government could address the problems the Task Force had identified. Frank and I agreed that he should constitute a second Task Force according to the same principles by which he had led the first. He could draw upon whomever he wished, inside or outside the government, without concern for representing any particular group or special interest. Apart from modest funds to hire student research assistants and draw upon consultants for specific expertise, he and other Task Force members were to serve without compensation and without being relieved from their other duties and responsibilities. The Task Force was to operate as openly as possible, involving all interested parties. Frank and I were in complete agreement that the Task Force's role should not be to represent HEW, but to develop constructive proposals which could be considered, within and without the government, as recommendations for federal action.

This document is the main report of the second Task Force. It integrates a series of proposals submitted to the Department by the Task Force. I commend it to the attention of federal officials throughout the Executive Depart-

ments and the Congress, and to all interested parties outside
government whose participation is indispensable to any
meaningful reexamination of the federal role in higher
education. Over the coming months, agency heads within
the Education Division of HEW will be reviewing this
proposal. We are interested in the comments and reactions
of all interested parties.

I would also like to acknowledge our appreciation to the
members of the Task Force and all those who participated
in their deliberations and contributed valued counsel in
the drafting and review of this second report. We are especially indebted to Frank Newman, whose refreshing views
and extraordinary energy have again enabled him to challenge us to reexamine existing policies in the light of
changing social needs.

S. P. Marland, Jr.
Assistant Secretary for Education

October 26, 1973

altered to take into account these developing problems?" Included in his concern were not only those problems identified in the first *Report* but those of other major commissions and task forces as well. He and the Commissioner of Education, Sidney Marland, soon to fill the new post of Assistant Secretary of Education, proposed the creation of a second Task Force to address these specific national policy questions and to transform the critique into a constructive program for national action.

This was an unusual step, but one based on an important principle. Secretary Richardson had discussed with us his perception of how change comes about, making plain the importance of national debate and discussion. He pointed out how easy it is for a task force to fall into the trap of believing that its job is to produce an intelligent document for the Secretary summing up in its view the wisdom available to that date, assuming that the Secretary then can and will push the necessary buttons to bring about whatever action is required. As the Secretary eloquently described to us, in the United States political action follows only when there is a broad perception that a problem exists, that there is a need to focus attention on that problem, and that rational solutions must be brought forward. As a result we went out both to generate policy proposals and to participate in the creation of that debate.

We were helped along by something unexpected: the remarkable response to the first report. As a result, we had a ready opportunity to follow the Secretary's suggestion. The members of the Task Force joined in the perilous but fascinating task of participating in a number of meetings around the country. The debate was not often about the

Preface

The work of this Task Force, including both the various position papers and this main report, *National Policy and Higher Education,* grew directly out of the work of an earlier Task Force which released its *Report on Higher Education* in 1971. When that first Task Force was created it was charged with examining the question posed by the then Secretary of HEW, Robert Finch: "How well does American higher education meet the needs of society in the 1970s?"

The *Report* noted that "The 1950s and 1960s were decades of unprecedented development and remarkable accomplishment in American education. There was a vast growth in numbers of students, faculty members, and facilities. Access to college widened steadily. Inequality of opportunity among economic classes and ethnic groups, long a factor preventing social mobility, was at last widely recognized as a national concern, and steps were taken toward correction. Greater opportunity was accorded each undergraduate to influence his own curriculum. Graduate education developed a level of scholarly excellence that became the envy of the world."

But, at the same time the *Report* noted that major problems had developed. The system of American higher education, as it had grown, had become more homogeneous and less flexible. "The system, with its massive inertia, resists fundamental change, rarely eliminates outmoded programs, ignores the differing needs of students, seldom questions its educational goals, and almost never creates new and different types of institutions."

By the time that the first Task Force reported, Elliot Richardson was Secretary of HEW. He raised a further question: "How can national policy and federal programs be

Report on Higher Education, but rather about the problems of higher education as we and others perceived them.

This report, *National Policy and Higher Education,* is a product, therefore, not only of the new research and analysis of the second Task Force, but of the participation of its members in that process of debate. We consciously drew into our work a great many knowledgeable people in higher education and in state and federal government, exposing the earlier drafts to them and gaining immensely from their pointed critiques.

Since the issues raised in the first *Report* are germane to this report, it might be well to review what they included.

In higher education, growth has been used traditionally as a measure of progress. . . . The common plea of educators is that this growth be nurtured until we reach the goal of access to a college education for every young American. . . . Yet access alone does not automatically lead to a successful education. . . . When the task force looked behind the growth statistics, they were found to mask a major phenomenon: the surprisingly large and growing number of students who voluntarily drop out of college. . . . [Attrition] figures indicate that of the more than one million young people who enter college each year, fewer than half will complete two years of study, and only about one-third will ever complete a four-year course of study.

While hundreds of thousands of students leave college because they find it disappointing, hundreds of thousands more enter and stay in when they might better serve their interests and aspirations elsewhere. Strong pressures in our society, some old, others recent, keep students in an academic lock-step of steadily longer duration—elementary school, high school, college, and graduate schools in unbroken succession.

American higher education is renowned for its diversity. Yet, in fact, our colleges and universities have become extraordinarily similar. Nearly all 2,500 institutions have adopted the same mode of teaching and learning. Nearly all strive to perform the same generalized educational mission. The traditional sources of differentiation—between public and private, large and small, secular and sectarian, male and female —are disappearing. Even the differences in character of individual institutions are fading. It is no longer true that most students have real choices among differing institutions in which to seek a higher education. . . . While the population seeking higher education is becoming ever more diverse—in class and social background, age, academic experience, and ability—our colleges and universities have come to assume that there is only one mode of teaching and learning—the academic mode. . . . Our Task Force has found some genuinely innovative approaches to teaching and learning. Yet the system of higher education tends to quarantine these innovative models so that, once started, they rarely spread.

As apprehension over the problem of college financing has become more acute, budgets have become the subject of increasing attention. But if the subject of the budget is more common on campus, the subject of cost effectiveness remains beyond the pale. The measurement of cost and performance in higher education is somehow regarded as illegitimate. . . . Thinking about costs is not simply a matter of paring budgets and making ends meet, of cutting out secretaries or not buying typewriters. It is a fundamental educational issue. . . . Thinking about cost effectiveness should be focused on particular learning situations. It should concern itself most with how the goals of a particular course or curriculum could most efficiently be achieved for particular kinds of students.

Commitment to the ideals of minority access to higher education is essential, but it is not enough—and least useful of all is a purely rhetorical commitment. In some measure, it is a matter of how much we are willing to invest. From our discussion with educational officers and the limited data available, it is obvious that the estimates made a few years ago of the cost of achieving effectively equal educational opportunity substantially understated the true amounts. It was a brave beginning back in the mid-sixties. But now the glamour has worn off and we are able to see more realistically the dimensions of the task ahead.

The higher education community prides itself on its leading role in the fight to end intolerance in American society. Yet with regard to women, colleges and universities practice a wide range of discriminatory practices. . . . The Task Force has identified three major types of barriers which block full participation by women in higher education: first, overt discrimination by faculties, deans, and others acting in official capacities; second, practical institutional barriers, such as rigid admission and residence requirements, and a lack of campus facilities and services, which makes participation in higher education incompatible with many women's other interests and activities; and third, the ingrained assumptions and inhibitions on the part of both men and women which deny the talents and aspirations of the latter.

Certification procedures—including the awarding of grades and degrees by colleges and universities—are a necessary part of our system of public protection and a convenience to everyone. But when the reliance on education credentials compels individuals to spend hours and years in schools against their interest, perpetuates social inequality, gives one group in society unique and arbitrary power over the lives of many, establishes conditions in which people will be dissatisfied and unhappy with their jobs, undermines the educational process, and all this unnecessarily—then the time has come to change these practices. There is an immediate need to break the credentials monopoly by opening up alternative routes to obtaining credentials. The monopolistic power of existing colleges and universities cannot be justified on the grounds of their effectiveness in screening for occupational performance, nor on the grounds that being the sole agencies for awarding degrees and credentials is necessary to their educational mission. New paths to certification are needed.

In the first report we commented that the hardest job for any task force is the identification of the key problems. Since completing the second report I would correct that initial impression. While identifying the critical issues is undoubtedly the most crucial aspect of reform, proposing concrete solutions to meet those challenges has proved substantially more

difficult. We hope our efforts will further stimulate the growing awareness of the problems and opportunities extant in
higher education and enliven the public discussion that gen-
erates productive reform.

November 16, 1973
Frank Newman

Letter of Transmittal

October 26, 1973

Hon. Sidney P. Marland, Jr.
Assistant Secretary for Education
Department of Health, Education, and Welfare
Washington, D.C. 20202

Dear Dr. Marland:

When the *Report on Higher Education* was released in March 1971, you asked that a second Task Force be created to recommend ways in which the federal government could address the problems identified in that report as well as the reports of other commissions and task forces. You asked that we proceed according to the principles which had governed the first Task Force; in particular, that the Task Force should proceed independently, openly, and with a clear understanding that we were speaking *to* the Department, rather attempting to speak *for* the Department.

In selecting a Task Force to meet this challenge, individuals were chosen for their ability to think creatively and constructively about the federal role in higher education. Several members of the first Task Force volunteered for the second effort, which ultimately comprised members from both institutions of higher education and various agencies of the federal government: the U.S. Office of Education; the Office of the Secretary of Health, Education, and Welfare; the Office of Management and Budget; and the professional staff of the Congress.

As we began our work, we found that many others, both within and outside the government, were willing to participate in the development of ideas, analysis of data, and criticism of drafts. Thus the Task Force has come to include a sizeable number of informal members, many of whom have participated fully in the generation of these recommendations. In addition to the members of the first Task Force formally appointed, Audrey Cohen and James Gibbons were kind enough to join fully in the deliberations of the second Task Force. As with the first Task Force, a great deal of the research and preparation of papers was done by interns and students—Trish Alexander, Michael Annison, Cathy Bernard, Martin Corry, Ruth Ann Crowley, William Diamond, Shirley Dixon, Patrick Dolan, Carolyn Ervin, Jackie Grover, William Holmer, Irma Johns, Kathryn Kopicki, Irene Lykes, Grady McGonagill, Lena Mitchell, Sina Morgan, John O'Leary, Theresa Rainer, Thyra Riley, Perry Saario, Carol Stoel, Don Tollefson, Philip Wu, Ted Youn.

We discovered early that generating recommendations for the various areas of federal involvement in higher education would require separate and detailed investigations and that prescription alone would not be sufficient. To help those involved to achieve responsible and enduring change, we believed we should accompany our proposals with a full statement of rationale, which could be made public and subjected to the scrutiny of interested constituencies outside as well as within the federal government. Thus we began the preparation of *policy papers* on various problem areas. Policy papers on Graduate Education, Data and Decision-Making in Higher Education, and a GI Bill for Community Service have already been released, and others are near completion.

In the course of developing these papers, we became convinced of the need to make explicit our perception of the new conditions affecting national policy, and our assumptions about the proper overall role of the federal government. We therefore prepared a central, integrative report to serve as an introduction to our policy papers, as a summary of our major recommendations, and as a statement of our general philosophy on the broad directions federal policy should take. We are pleased to present you with this report, *National Policy and Higher Education.*

Though it is the product of extensive discussion and criticism within the Task Force, and among many knowledgeable people in postsecondary education, we have no illusions that it is a definitive statement. Rather, we hope it can serve as a vehicle for a continuing and constructive debate, within and outside the government.

We owe you a special vote of thanks. At every stage of this effort, you have supported without hesitation the idea of analysis and discussion as central to the ongoing process of renewal of our national education policy. It has been a privilege for each of us to be involved with you.

Sincerely,

Frank Newman
Robert Andringa
William Cannon
Christopher Cross
Don Davies
Russell Edgerton
Martin Kramer
Bernie Martin

Attachment

Introduction

In the 1950s and 1960s, our nation made an unprecedented commitment to extend opportunities for higher education to a large portion of the American population. Now, in the decade of the 1970s, we are challenged by the consequences of this commitment. American higher education has developed a dedication to social equity and individual opportunity as well as a level of excellence in scholarship unmatched in our own history or in the world. But problems of the most fundamental nature are yet to be faced.

The expansion of enrollments has created demands that higher education fulfill a new social purpose. When higher education served only the few, it was sufficient to identify those among the few who had academic talent and prepare them for positions of social and professional leadership. But now that over half of all young Americans as well as millions of older Americans are entering some form of college, higher education has assumed a new purpose—that of actually educating all who enter so that each individual might fulfill his or her own potential. The implications of this new social purpose for the process of education are enormous.

As the numbers of students entering and graduating from higher education has expanded, it has become harder and harder for colleges to guarantee to their graduates privileged entry into careers of high status and income. Thus, the new relationship developing between college-going and mobility is making it necessary to rethink why individuals should attend college, and why society should invest such a sizeable share of its resources in higher education.

Expanded enrollments have brought to higher education a population which is not only larger than before, but far more diverse. It includes individuals from socioeconomic, ethnic, and age groups previously underrepresented. It includes millions of individuals with differing goals and differing styles of learning. This, in turn, has created an urgent need for a greater diversity of paths to a college education and for a broader range of educational services. The rapidly expanding range of programs of higher education different from those of the traditional colleges and universities is only now being recognized as forming a broad expanse called "postsecondary education," the boundaries of which are still unclear.

Finally, expanded enrollments have led to a twelve-fold increase in expenditures on higher education in the past twenty-five years. This, in turn, has led to increased public and governmental interest in higher education, to growing demands for performance and accountability, and to new forms of organization and decision-making. Increasingly, institutions are becoming enveloped in a larger system of relationships with multicampus central offices and statewide agencies. Increasingly, the process of higher education is becoming entangled in a thicket of bureaucratic regulation—from professional and accrediting agencies, unions, the courts, state governments, and the federal government.

None of the implications of these conditions have yet been extensively debated or accepted as premises for a new national policy toward postsecondary education.

Indeed, not since Sputnik has the American public engaged in a thoughtful, extensive discussion of the national interest in postsecondary education. Student unrest became an important *political* issue in the late 1960s, as did the question of access for minority students. In the early 1970s, the institutions of higher education themselves raised the issue of their state of *financial* distress. Yet none of these issues provoked a thoughtful debate about national *educational* policy.

The closest contemporary analogy to the catalytic force of Sputnik was the debate leading up to the passage of the Education Amendments of 1972. The need to reauthorize federal legislation created a major political struggle over the directions of federal student assistance and the merits of initiating new general federal support to institutions of higher education. Yet even such a fundamental revision of the federal role as this was debated only among a narrow circle of interested educational and political leaders. A temporary agreement on the nature of the federal role was achieved, but fundamental issues were deferred, and a new commission to study the financing of postsecondary education was created to establish a forum for further analysis. A new deadline for the determination of national postsecondary education policy occurs in less than two years, when current legislation will expire.

More important, however, than deadlines for legislative action is the fact that across the country states and institutions are moving past the point of no return on crucial decisions. Those decisions are being and will be made, but often by default. In particular, the drift toward centralized and detailed controls could, unless they are thoughtfully analyzed and new means are found for accountability, undermine the capacity of the institutions of higher education to remain responsive and capable of adapting to changing conditions.

We believe there is an urgent need for a debate of these issues, not just in Washington, but in the state capitals and on every campus. It is with this in mind that the Task Force makes its recommendations. The report focuses on the role of the federal government as the chief vehicle for the expression of the national interest in postsecondary education; but it is addressed not only to federal officials but to all those concerned with questions of national educational leadership.

Two overriding themes dominate this report. First, in addition to supporting access to college, and subsidizing research and manpower training in various areas, the federal government must shift its concern from encouraging growth to a new concern for *effectiveness* throughout postsecondary education.

Second, the federal government must develop a new concern for the form of public support, for the manner in which decisions are made, and for the purposes to be achieved, in order to preserve conditions under which postsecondary education can remain viable and responsive. Attention and analysis must be focused not only on the *levels* of public support for postsecondary education, but on the *purposes* and *forms* of federal and state involvement as well.

Higher education is not, and should never become, a "system" like those established for compulsory education at the elementary and secondary levels. Higher education is a set of institutions voluntarily attended by individuals who have different talents and abilities and who seek different things from their educational experience. These institutions are already more homogeneous in their missions and academic programs and more uniform in their teaching and administrative procedures than they should be if they are to maximize their effectiveness as centers of thought and learning. Thus, perhaps our greatest challenge in the 1970s will be to develop forms of public support and accountability, based not on the image of common institutions providing common educational experiences, but on the image of differentiated institutions reaching out for ever more effective approaches to serve an increasingly diverse clientele.

1
The Implications of the
Egalitarian Commitment

It is one thing to espouse equal access to college as a goal toward which the nation strives. It is another thing entirely to deal with the implications of that policy as a reality. Today, American society has largely achieved the goal of access, but has yet to make the adjustments in public policy necessary for an era of realistic mass educational opportunities.

Three Eras of Social Purpose in Higher Education[1]

For a long period following the founding of the first colleges, higher education in this country, as in Europe, could be described as *aristocratic,* being essentially devoted to receiving the children of the well-to-do and making of them a competent class of business leaders, professionals, teachers, clergy, and government officers.

What made higher education in America more democratic than in Europe was the year-by-year expansion of access and the ease with which new colleges could be founded. Any well-organized group could, if excluded from the establishment of the day, found a college with its own specific mission.[2] The beginnings of public higher education, with the founding of institutions such as City University of New York in the urban centers or the land-grant colleges in the newly settled areas, opened further opportunities.[3]

Still, it is important to keep in mind that by 1900 only about one in twenty-five young Americans entered college.[4] While several of the major state universities had open access, it was more open in theory than in fact. Though any high school graduate was eligible for entrance, most denied themselves the opportunity by assuming they were not academically or socially "college material," and of those who chose to enter, a sizeable proportion was flunked out.[5]

Steadily the aristocratic concept weakened, and by the 1930s, American higher education was well into its second, or *meritocratic* period.[6] Colleges increasingly sought to select able students whatever their background, and make of them a new elite based not on birth but on talent. In 1954, one commission summarized this revised attitude: "The nation needs to make effective use of its intellectual resources. To do so means to use well its brightest people whether they come from farm or city, from the slum section or the country club area, regardless of color or religious or economic differences *but not regardless of ability*." [7]

After World War II, the spread of meritocratic values accelerated, and simultaneously the concept of merit became closely tied to that of ability as measured by narrowly academic forms of grading and testing. Colleges and universities began to sort themselves according to the quality of their research and the selectivity of their admissions policies. Such selectivity required much wider use of nationally-normed tests and other means of rejecting applicants than had previously been the case.

Meritocratic values, as measured by grades and test scores, still dominate. But by the middle 1960s, higher education began moving into a third period, one which might be called *egalitarian*. Increasingly, the American public has assumed that everyone should have a chance at a college education. In addition to educating meritorious students who have demonstrated a narrowly *academic* potential, colleges are now expected to give each individual a chance to fulfill his or her *individual* potential. The goal has become, in the terms put forward in one widely noted statement, to "make the national purpose serve the human purpose: that every person shall have the opportunity to become all that he or she is capable of becoming. We believe that knowledge is essential to individual freedom and to the conduct of a free society. We believe that education is the surest and most profitable investment a nation can make." [8]

Participation in American postsecondary education is still far from being universal. Access rates still differ significantly by socioeconomic status and by state.[9] But numerous milestones mark progress toward egalitarian goals:

A continual rise in the rate of college attendance, to the point where more than 50 percent (and in some states more than 70 percent) of young Americans enter some institution of higher education.[10]

The development of community colleges, which now enroll over two and a half million students.[11]

The response in the 1960s to the needs of minorities, almost doubling their enrollment since 1967.[12]

The opening of new institutions focused specifically on the needs of the least advantaged, including those based on newly noticed ethnic groups.[13]

The decision of the City University of New York in 1970 to provide open access to institutions beyond the community college level.[14]

The establishment of open universities to create new opportunities for students unable to attend a conventional campus.[15]

A shift of public interest in student aid from a concern solely with students of high academic ability (through programs such as the National Merit Scholars) to a concern with helping those in economic need (through programs such as Educational Opportunity Grants).[16]

New federal legislation implying that all young Americans are *entitled* to financial assistance for postsecondary opportunities.[17]

As the interest of society shifts toward egalitarian goals, new and profound issues of public educational policy are raised. What is the responsibility of society toward those students for whom the traditional style of teaching and learning is not appropriate? How do we judge an individual's progress or an institution's success? Where access must be restricted, on what basis should selections be made? What kinds of educational experiences in what types of institutions should be recognized as a legitimate part of postsecondary education?

Given their importance in higher education, federal policies concerning the eligibility of students and institutions for assistance, the level of resources to be provided, the accreditation of institutions, and the development of tests for evaluating student performance must all be altered to reflect the new realities of public philosophy toward postsecondary education.

Access Alone Is Not Enough
As equality of opportunity was understood in the 1950s and 1960s, both the college and society were given relatively limited roles: The role of the college was to be available to those who met its standards; that of society was to provide the funds for new colleges and for student aid. Criteria for success and failure were based on the entry of, but not necessarily the education of, the individual student.

This minimal formulation of equality of opportunity, however, turned out to be as difficult in practice as it was simple in theory. The mass of students were given a chance to compete, but within the framework of goals and rules adapted from institutions designed to serve a much more limited group of students. Access for new students was soon followed by attrition. For example, despite the avowed intention of three-fourths of the entering freshmen at the new community colleges to obtain a bachelor's degree, only about one-third complete even a two-year program, and even fewer transfer to a four-year college.[18]

To close the gap between public philosophy and educational performance, the national concern must move beyond a focus on access to a concern with the *effectiveness* of the educational process in relation to the individual. But what are realistic goals for an increasingly egalitarian era? First, we believe there are some goals which are *not* appropriate.

The goal cannot be equality of results,[19] for students have differing needs, aims, and abilities. In elementary education, there is a broad social purpose served by encouraging students to develop common skills—mastery of the language, knowledge of civics, familiarity with mathematics—and to share common social experiences. But even here, in a system depending on compulsory attendance, with common textbooks, with the student as the directed party, and with carefully structured age progressions, equality of results seems an elusive goal.

Postsecondary education cannot attempt to approximate the unity of the common school. Postsecondary education is a group of institutions attended on a voluntary basis. Students come not only with differing abilities and motivations, but with differing goals. How can there be equality of results between an 18-year-old student studying nursing to prepare for a career and a 40-year-old, fully engaged in a career, studying psychology in order to develop a new and broader outlook toward life? Even among 18-year-olds studying the same subjects, equality of results cannot be achieved through uniformity of experience, for the students' differences in abilities and styles of learning cannot be normed to produce a uniform experience.

Nor should the push toward egalitarianism and the new interest in applying systematic management to the governance of postsecondary education lead to a uniformity of societal inputs. There is in the present political climate a danger of inadvertent leveling. Graduate education does cost more than undergraduate, just as teaching physics costs more than history, vocational education more than liberal arts, medicine more than training in law. This does not mean that postsecondary education should train all historians and no physicists, all liberal arts majors and no computer technicians, all lawyers and no doctors. Incentives are needed to make *all* programs more effective in their use of resources, but one should look for differing results and expect differing costs.

While public policy cannot have as a goal equality of results and should not have as a goal equality of inputs, we believe it should encourage much more than just access to some institution labeled "college." What we believe *is* an appropriate goal of public policy beyond that of access, is the provision of an opportunity for more meaningful choices among *many* forms of postsecondary education. Particularly for those whose educational capabilities and interests do not square with the existing institutions, this must go beyond the simpler concept of equality of access put forward a decade ago. It requires the resolution of a set of difficult new issues.

The New Domain of Postsecondary Education
It used to be easier to define what constituted higher education. There were colleges, universities, and vocational schools. "Higher education" meant the education given in

the first two classes of institutions; and the term "college student" was applied only to one attending these institutions. Today the spectrum from research university to proprietary vocational school is close to continuous, and a new term, "postsecondary education," has come into use to encompass this broader range of institutions, difficult as it is to fix the limits of that term.

As community colleges developed, encompassing both liberal arts from the traditional college and vocational studies from the vocational or technical schools, the old distinctions began to blur. The acceptance of the community college as a "college" has led, in turn, to a new opportunity for legitimacy for proprietary schools.[20] It is difficult to see why someone should not be a legitimate "student" while studying computer programming at a proprietary school if someone else is a "student," counted in the national statistics and eligible for state or federal student aid, because he is studying computer programming at a community college. Both types of institutions have been growing rapidly— much more rapidly than the traditional four-year colleges and universities. Today there are more than 1,100 community college campuses with over two and a half million students and more than 10,000 proprietary schools enrolling almost two million students.[21]

Concurrently, there has been a movement toward non-traditional studies. Campus-based colleges such as Goddard, the University of South Florida, Brigham Young University, Roosevelt University, or the State University at Brockport, have established external programs for non-campus-based students. (A few, such as the University of Oklahoma, have had them for years.) Now, non-campus-based or "open" learning systems such as Empire State, Minnesota Metro, or the University Without Walls have been established and many more are on the drawing boards.[22]

Research institutes such as the Rand Corporation and Arthur D. Little have begun granting degrees. Large corporations such as Xerox, Motorola, IBM, or GE have developed extensive educational centers. The Department of Agriculture Graduate School provides opportunities for continuing education for federal employees and others. The Armed Forces operate a geographically dispersed and educationally diverse system. The College Entrance Examination Board has announced a program to help libraries become learning centers where adults can earn credits toward college degrees. A number of newspapers are conducting a program in American studies for which readers will be able to obtain credit at cooperating colleges. Education for personal development and cultural enrichment is offered by still other institutions—language schools, zoological gardens, or the Esalen Institute. The total enrollment in all programs beyond high school has been estimated to be as high as 50 or 60 million.[23]

How much of this should be encompassed by the term "postsecondary education"? How should the federal government determine what is beyond the pale, ineligible for participation in programs of student aid, institutional support, or research funding? Which institutions and students should be included in the federal statistics, or affected by federal regulation? Surely not every institution that claims to educate someone should be eligible.

We believe that the recognized universe of postsecondary education must be broad in an era of egalitarianism, and that the old domain of higher education is not broad enough for the education of the present spectrum of students. The relationship between accrediting and eligibility for federal funds must be redefined to meet today's circumstances.[24] Federal statistics and the national concern must encompass many of the newly recognized institutions.[25]

Excellence in an Egalitarian Era

As the number of students increases and as the domain of postsecondary education becomes broader, there is a growing concern among educators that all this will lead to a lowering of academic standards. We agree that unless some serious thinking is done, the drive for more open opportunity may well result in a dilution of standards.[26] But no matter how egalitarian postsecondary education becomes, a striving for measures of excellence is essential for effectiveness. In consideration of the new goals of postsecondary education, how is excellence to be measured for the institution and for the student?

Much of the measuring of both—at least for undergraduate education—presently rests on a myth, according to which excellence is determined by selective admission and amount of time spent "in residence" (measured in terms of credit hours). For the best institutions this is a reasonably safe approach since they are almost certain to get out what they put in, bright students, and are hardly likely to be criticized on those grounds. But even the institutions most skilled at this practice, the great research universities, do not follow these same standards for measuring the two activities they regard as critical—scholarly research and the awarding of major graduate or professional degrees. Measurement of the quality of research depends instead upon peer review and competitive grants. Few universities would be prepared to award major graduate degrees on the basis of the piling up of a sufficient number of credit hours without some supplemental individual test of professional competency such as is provided by oral exams, dissertations, clinical rounds, or moot court competitions.

When only a small percentage of the age group entered college, the time-based system probably did no major harm, since most students were fully able to educate themselves despite its limitations. But, as more and more of the age group enters college, the continuance of the time-based, credit hour system of measurement will mean that soon only persistence will matter in the attainment of a degree. Gradually it will become apparent to all that such a standard for educational credentials is not relevant; and, in fact, attacks on the current value of a degree have already begun.[27]

We believe it is inappropriate to try to preserve the old system. Rather, it is time to begin the shift away from a time-based system as a measure of the progress of the student, and away from a dependence on selectivity in admissions as a measure of the effectiveness of the institutions.[28] We do believe there must be measures of excellence; but in an educational community as broad and diverse as that which now exists, there must be *many* measures, each of which is relevant to the students and institutions for which it is used.

Judging Institutional Effectiveness

The social purpose which is ascribed to college has profound implications for determining what colleges should do and how well they are succeeding. Colleges today are judged as effective or ineffective based on the selectivity of their admissions process and the share of their graduating class gaining admission to the best graduate schools. A regular pyramid of institutional prestige has evolved: The great research universities are arranged in order at the top (their place is assured because of both their selectivity in admissions and the prestige which the academic world accords research and the granting of doctoral degrees). Then come the selective four-year colleges, followed by the state colleges. Community colleges barely make the bottom of the pyramid, while proprietary institutions are not even mentioned in polite academic society.

An ironic reminder of the irrelevance of all this to the question of education at the graduate level occurred in 1970. That year the American Council on Education's periodic survey of graduate education, based on the judgment of university faculty peers around the country, reported that the French Department at the University of California, Berkeley, was fifth in the nation in "Quality of Graduate Faculty" and eighth in "Effectiveness of Doctoral Program." During the same year, the University of California system itself issued a scathing report implying that the French Department was consciously misleading Ph.D. candidates and was structured to exploit both graduate and undergraduate students. Interestingly, neither report addressed the question of whether a graduate student in that department learned anything that later correlated with his or her effectiveness as a teacher or a scholar in French.[29]

In assessing the fulfillment of egalitarian objectives, one must not merely look to the quality of the college's graduates, which may indicate only that it has recruited academically able freshmen, but, rather, one must look to the contribution the college makes to the development of the student's abilities. What is the *educational value added?* A community college which helps bring about significant changes in students of lower initial skills should be judged more effective than a prestigious university which does little more than admit able students and graduate them undamaged four years later. A selective college or university should be judged effective only if it excels at the further intellectual and social development of the already-talented.[30]

We believe that there must be many pyramids, not just one. The great research universities of this country are essential to the nation's life. Competition among them in education and research based on relevant measures of excellence is crucial. But theirs is not the only task. Just as it is impossible to compare the social contribution of an outstanding chemist with that of a leading lawyer, so one cannot, and need not, compare Yale or Wisconsin with Medgar Evers or Evergreen State. Of each we should demand excellence, but measured against *different* and *relevant* standards.

Judging Individual Performance

Just as a broader spectrum of students was gaining access to higher education, the measures of selection and evaluation were becoming increasingly focused on narrow concepts of academic ability. The resulting contradiction between broader access and narrower standards of measurement led to an emphasis on academic sorting—the use of grades and tests to select the students who would be able to compete on these grounds for entrance to graduate or prestigious undergraduate programs. In turn, a further result was the reinforcement of a narrow view of the process of education, focused on the organization of the transfer of knowledge into academic disciplines.[31] As higher education has become more egalitarian, grading has become less a measure of a student's educational progress and more a means of shunting aside those students who do not fit easily into the academic world.

Aptitude tests, originally intended to help standardize and simplify admissions procedures, were adapted to this screening process. Whereas during the 1920s and 1930s the yearly increase in the number of people taking tests for college entrance was slight, after World War II their use began to jump—from 25,000 tests given in 1945 to half a million in 1960, and to almost 2 million by 1970.[32] Concurrently, the grade point average became the all-important measure —not of learning but of one's opportunity for advancement along the academic ladder. Only in the last twenty years, with the flood of new students, has the concept of academic selectivity become firmly established. Not only did Harvard, Yale, Princeton, and Stanford become "selective"; so did Michigan, Berkeley, and North Carolina.[33]

But, for years, the idea that the accomplishment of the student and the effectiveness of the institution can be measured by narrow types of grades and tests has been under attack, and the intensity of that attack has been growing.[34] It must be noted that grades and tests in their present forms *do* predict performance at the next level of education. They *do* in certain ways motivate the student. And because of the artificial restrictions built in by educators and employers, grades *do* influence who gets the economic, social, and political rewards of our society.[35]

Unfortunately, however, grades are most often used to measure one's ability to repeat uncritically information in the same form as it was received. Assembly-line education has made grading and testing less a measure of the student's development and more a rite of passage required for entrance to the next level of education. No other measures for evaluating the progress of students are in widespread use.[36] For most students, contact with the faculty is minimal, averaging less than twenty minutes per quarter outside class.[37] The continuing focus on the current measures rewards the conforming plodder at the expense of creativity, depth, and subtlety.[38] Beyond that, studies of businessmen, doctors, policemen, teachers, engineers, air traffic controllers, bank tellers, factory workers, dentists, and even scholars indicate, in the words of one researcher, that grades and tests "bear little or no relationship to any measures of adult accomplishment." [39] Thus grades are related to who gains the status of having received a college degree but they do not seem to predict performance beyond schooling.

Today the race is to the academically swift. But as society and postsecondary education become more egalitarian, the issue cannot be simply how a student compares with his peers. Rather, increasing importance must be placed on questions of the individual student's potential: how far he has developed in terms of his potential, what he wants to do, and how the college can assist him.[40]

This is not to say that the comparative measure of merit is not important. There are, by any standards, great differences in the abilities of individuals, and these should be recognized.[41] But human ability is multidimensional, while much of present testing is one-dimensional and fails to take into account the fact that different students use differing abilities to learn and develop. Even worse, current testing practices often fail to measure those very characteristics traditionally considered central in the process of a liberal education: the ability to think critically, to organize in order to accomplish a task, to tolerate ambiguity and differing points of view, to master the process of learning—all those characteristics which insure the usefulness of the student's education in life beyond the academy. Attempts to measure the progress of the student in his intellectual and social development over time are almost nonexistent.[42]

Not only does this leave the student with no useful yard-stick for self-guidance, but the institution, unable to gauge the needs of its students, also finds it difficult to change and adapt in order to improve its educational impact on the particular category of students it serves. Research studies, as well as the experience of a number of colleges willing to experiment, such as Ottawa University, Stirling College, or Eckert College, have shown that coursework and grading can be restructured to accelerate student development.[43] It should also be noted that these issues have become a matter of concern to many admissions officers at selective institutions and at some graduate schools, as well as to the national testing agencies which have been developing new forms of testing for differing dimensions of intellectual growth. But much more work needs to be done.[44]

Measures of individual merit are essential, but if they are to be useful in measuring educational progress and to be equitable in the allocation of opportunities, they must be related to the stated purposes of education. New means for measuring the student's intellectual growth must be developed.[45]

Who Gets In When Access Is Limited?
As more and more individuals seek ever higher levels of education, what are the grounds for selecting some over others? In undergraduate education, the response to the

demand for access has been to expand the number of places to accommodate almost everyone. There is still an important question as to who gets into the most selective colleges and universities, but the admissions decisions of these institutions are not all-or-nothing matters to the student—there are always other places to go for a bachelor's degree.

A more difficult situation arises in the case of specialized or graduate training. Expanding to create a place for everyone is not rational in terms of the resources needed or the potential career openings requiring such training. With more qualified applicants than places, selections must and should be made on the basis of merit. But merit of what kind?

We believe that traditional academic measures should be supplemented by standards which predict successful performance *beyond* schooling.[46] In some fields this has always been done. Although both intelligence and a broad cultural background are likely to be useful to a concert musician or an actor, it is not common to use grades or nationally-normed tests to select entrants to conservatories or actors' workshops. For a potential physician, however, high school grades are essential for entrance to a selective undergraduate college—where grades become even more essential for entrance to medical school.[47] Yet those grades predict little if anything of the student's interest in or qualifications for service to other people.

If medical schools and other graduate schools and their students were entirely privately supported, the issue might be of less direct concern. But, in most graduate departments, the student's tuition pays only a fraction of the costs and public support is significant. Often the student receives some form of public assistance toward his tuition and other costs as well. Surely the purpose of public support must be to assist in the selection and training of those practitioners in each field who will be most useful to society *after graduation*. It is, therefore, a matter of significant national interest to develop new means of selection, measurements of the results of education, and ways of coupling these to probable postgraduate achievement.[48]

The goals of American society for education beyond high school have changed. A broader range of citizens from diverse backgrounds with diverse skills now seeks an education. A broader range of institutions comprising what is now called postsecondary education seeks to serve them.

We believe that much of that broader range of institutions should be recognized as a legitimate part of the educational community. Rather than leading to a weakening or elimination of standards, the new egalitarian drive should lead to different and more useful standards. Whether a student has high intellectual skills is important; but whether the process of education is helping students of every level of skill to further their intellectual development is even more important.

Federal policies with regard to accrediting, the collection of statistics, student aid, and the sponsorship of educational research influence almost every aspect of the extent of the domain of postsecondary education and the nature of its standards. These policies must now be readjusted to reflect the realities of the nation's commitment to an egalitarian era.

2
The End of Guaranteed
Social Mobility

Americans have long considered college as the gateway to the upper middle class. For those seeking upward social mobility for themselves or for their children, the American model is no longer the self-made man but the university graduate.[1]

Students who are the first generation in their families to go to college are especially attracted to the diploma as an admission ticket to social and career territory not realistically accessible to their parents.[2] It is ironic but inevitable that, just as college opportunities are finally within reach of so many new students, the colleges are losing their capacity for social and occupational placement. Because so many have been to college, a college education is now a necessary but no longer sufficient condition for social mobility. Not having the degree may block opportunities, but having it will not ensure them.

Public Expectations of Status and Income

The effort to expand access coupled with a steady stream of rhetoric from the educational community and government has tended to reinforce widespread expectations that there is a direct relationship between the amount of education and the likelihood of upward mobility in status and income. It is no wonder that students and their parents readily make this connection, when institutions of higher education put it forward in news releases, catalogues, and in one recent case, even on billboards.[3] College degrees, it has been pointed out repeatedly, are worth a great deal to the student over his lifetime.

Federal pronouncements also support this supposition. A Veterans Administration circular, encouraging veterans' use

of the GI Bill, recently claimed that "college graduates have
an average lifetime income that is $237,000 more than per-
sons with only a high school diploma—$608,000 compared
to $371,000." [4] Advocates of federal aid policies have as-
sumed, based on a study of that GI Bill, that a modest investment in student aid yields substantial returns in higher
taxes.

Obviously there is some relationship between a college
degree and relatively high status and income. One expects
social status to be related to higher education partly because
of the prestige of simply being a college graduate, partly because degrees are required for entry into certain careers, and
partly because the skills that can be acquired in college are
generally useful in life.[5] What limited evidence there is
indicates that there is a relationship, but how direct, how
universal, and how causal it is have been badly exagger-
ated.[6] Those who attend college are more likely to be up-
wardly mobile compared to their parents than those who
do not attend college, are more likely to earn higher incomes, are more likely to vote, less likely to be on welfare,
and less likely to have mental health problems.[7] But what
is cause and what is effect?

Many of these results, perhaps most, occur not because of
the effects of college, but because a great many bright, aggressive, well-balanced and socially interested people perceive the value of going to college in this society and act
upon that perception.

But some of the results are ambiguous. There are clearly
more high earners who went to college and more low earners who have never gone to college, but in between are
about 60 percent of the wage earners for whom college and

noncollege incomes are indistinguishable.[8] And some part of these results comes from credentialism—from the arbitrary use of degrees to screen job candidates.

But perhaps the most important question is whether the traditional assumptions about college as a route to higher social status and income can remain valid as more and more Americans enter college.

Oversupply and Underemployment

Within the last few years, it has become apparent that in many occupations traditionally reserved for college graduates, the numbers completing their training are outrunning the normal opportunities for employment. An early problem was the relationship between supply and demand for Ph.D.'s in physics, later in the supply of all Ph.D.'s relative to new openings for faculty members.[9] Then came the oversupply of engineers, and still more recently overcrowding in such fields as elementary and secondary teaching and even law.[10] Increasingly, the question arises whether the job market can provide sufficiently challenging—and high-paying—positions for all these well-trained people.

An oversupply of college graduates has rarely before been a problem; rather, it has been common to hear just the opposite concern. One report published in the mid-1960s raised the question "whether technological progress may induce a demand for very skilled and highly-educated people in numbers our society cannot yet provide, while at the same time leaving stranded many of the unskilled and poorly-educated with no future opportunities for employment." [11]

There is strong evidence that the current problems plaguing job-seeking graduates are *not* temporary phenomena, but will continue to be a fact of life throughout the

1970s. In the aggregate, technology creates more jobs than it destroys, but the jobs created do not always require more skill than those replaced.[12] For the last few years, this problem has been compounded by an economic recession and a slowdown in the flow of research and development funds, especially in aerospace and defense, which have combined to lessen the demand for college-trained employees just as that supply was reaching new peaks.[13] But with the rapid growth in college-going, the trained manpower supply has long since met the demand in almost all fields.

The actual requirements of the economy for trained manpower are extraordinarily difficult to measure.[14] Requirements for new levels of education to perform effectively the tasks of an increasingly sophisticated society have become hard to distinguish from the arbitrary redefinition of jobs to require higher levels of education because of the availability of college-trained applicants. For example, it is increasingly common now for policemen to have had college training, and for some police and correctional work at least two years of college is now a requirement. Is this because the role of the policeman is becoming more complex, or is it because there are enough applicants with such training that the employer can do a preliminary sorting by establishing such requirements? [15] No doubt there is an element of both as well as a new perception on society's part of the need for self-esteem in such roles.

Two clues may help measure the extent of the surplus. First, in the simplest terms, at the current levels of college attendance, each year the economy must absorb new graduates into the job market in approximately twice the proportion as currently exists in the total work force;[16] and it must absorb in even larger proportion new entrants who have attended college but are not graduates. Even if one assumes that entry-level jobs require a somewhat higher proportion of college-educated people than the whole of the work force, an assumption for which we have no evidence, this is an extraordinary jump.

Second, compared to other sophisticated societies in the developed world, such as West Germany, Sweden, or Japan, the American economy already absorbs at least twice the percentage of college graduates as the next nation, and again an even larger share of nongraduate college attendees. In other words, we currently absorb twice the percentage of college graduates into the work force as our nearest economic competitor, a cumulative total for the American work force of about 14%; and, at current graduation rates, the percentage must soon double again, to about 25%.[17]

Many assume that the trend toward more education simply matches a shift in the nature of the work force as the United States moves into a postindustrial knowledge economy. Table 1 shows the ten- and twenty-year shifts in the division of the total work force into occupational groups.[18]

With regard to the two main "college-type" job categories, "professional and technical" has grown by 6.7% from 1950 to 1970, while "managers, officials, proprietors" has *declined* by 0.2%. But during these same twenty years, college attendance for the age group reaching 18 to 22 has increased from less than 20 percent to over 50 percent.[19] In the largest professional category, teaching, for which traditionally more than a third of the bachelor's candidates prepare, the number of new openings is expected to decline over the rest of the decade. Yet this year there were 243,000 beginning teachers competing for 132,000 positions. The less fortunate 111,000 do not simply disappear, but in turn enter the com-

Table 1. Percent Distribution of Employment by Major Occupational Groups

	1950[a]	1960[b]	1970[b]
White collar	37.5	43.4	48.3
Professional and technical	7.5	11.4	14.2
Managers, officials, proprietors	10.8	10.7	10.5
Clerical	12.8	14.8	17.4
Sales	6.4	6.4	6.2
Blue collar	39.1	36.6	35.3
Craftsmen, foremen	12.9	13.0	12.9
Operatives	20.3	18.2	17.7
Nonfarm labor	5.9	5.4	4.7
Service	11.0	12.2	12.4
Private household	3.2	3.0	2.0
Other services	7.8	9.2	10.4
Farm	12.5	7.9	4.0
Farmers and managers	7.4	4.2	2.2
Farm laborers and foremen	5.1	3.3	1.7

a. Persons 14 years of age and over

b. Persons 16 years of age and over

Source: *Manpower Report to the President*, 1971; and *Statistical Supplement to the Manpower Report to the President*, 1965.

petition for other "college-type" jobs. The result of all this has been a steady increase in the number of college graduates and college attendees showing up in other categories, particularly in "clerical," "sales," and "other services." [20]

In the short run, balancing supply and demand for well-trained manpower is even more difficult than even these figures imply. The discussion above understates the growth in postsecondary education because it does not reflect the increase in older students returning to college or the growth in enrollment in postsecondary education outside the colleges and universities.[21] It also fails to account for the changing perception of the role of women.

Twenty years ago, most women graduating from college expected to become full-time wives and mothers. Those that entered the labor force were required to settle for jobs that normally demanded less than a college education. The case of the Phi Beta Kappa from Radcliffe or Vassar who finally managed to land a secretarial post at a New York publishing house has become a part of the folklore. Only in teaching and nursing did women have ready access to professional jobs.

1971 was a watershed year. For the first time, more than half the women between 18 and 64 (and over 40 percent of the married women) in this country were in the paid labor force.[22] And, increasingly, women are demanding full equality, backed by the legal powers of the federal government and encouraged by such developments as the advertising program of the National Organization of Women. Since women currently receive 43 percent of the bachelor's degrees granted in this country,[23] the trend toward their entering the work force with new and higher expectations, just as their traditional professional occupation (teaching) has begun to contract, sharply increases the number of graduates competing for the better jobs.

By the end of the 1970s, the problem may be less severe, as every year a smaller number of Americans will turn eighteen.[24] By that time also, both the structure of the work force and public expectations may well have undergone considerable change.[25] And none of this means that large numbers of unemployed college graduates will be walking the streets. There will be more "good" jobs than ever before and the most promising graduates will do better than ever.[26]

But, as the supply of college graduates expands, mere possession of a degree, particularly in the liberal arts and humanities, will not be sufficient to land what has been considered an appropriate job. Assuming the same steady but modest rate of growth of knowledge-demanding jobs as has been true through the last two decades, we believe that, *in terms of traditional expectations,* there will be a general underemployment of many college graduates.

College-Going and Downward Mobility

The increase in college-going leads inevitably to a dilemma. While American society has been remarkably adept at expanding its middle class, mobility is naturally perceived in relationship to someone else. If many are moving up then some must move down—at least relatively. Clearly not everyone can become a member of the upper middle class. There are, in fact, two important trends which appear to run counter to the traditional perception of college attendance as leading to increased social status and its assumed companions, a "college-type" job and an increased income.

For some children of middle or upper class families, college-going fails to keep them from *downward* social mobility. Recently much press attention has been focused on a few individuals in this category—the taxi driver from Harvard or the Berkeley graduate living in a woodsy commune.[27] While they may represent the attention-getting fringe, there does seem to be a significant and growing trend toward downward mobility. Though middle and upper class children usually have an advantage in the quality of school they attend and often in their intellectual training in the home, not all are academically motivated or skilled. A significant percentage become college dropouts.[28] In addition, as more of the population enters college, the competition for the "good" jobs increases, leading to an increased importance for such additional attributes as motivation, personality, and experience. Some children of the middle or upper class who have attended college are uninterested in conventional careers, and others are either unwilling or unable to face the competition.[29]

With the decline of aristocratic assumptions and the rise of an emphasis on training and credentials, it has become more difficult to pass on status. Illustrative of this phenomenon is the case recently described to the Task Force of a couple, both of whom are well-known scholars.[30] Their combined income (added to, in this case, some inherited wealth), as well as their positions and reputations, place them clearly in the upper class. Both children are college dropouts, one working in a lumber yard, the other a waitress. Their parents can, with the current inheritance taxes, pass on money —but not position. They can insure access to college[31] but not the fruits of college. The same is true for that traditional American, the corner druggist (nowadays the manager of a drugstore chain) who can no longer pass on his position, his degree in pharmacy, or his license. Increasingly, the crucial question is whether the parents pass on the motivation to succeed *at something*.

The second trend is the new ability for many to bypass college to reach *middle income* in jobs that do not require college training and which have not historically been viewed as *middle class*. Many teamsters, longshoremen, and construction workers earn between $15,000 and $20,000 a year —twice the median wage-earner's income.[32]

College, therefore, though it does provide an edge, is not a certain route to riches, nor is it the only route. We believe that this will help create a more meritocratic society, but one based on standards other than those currently being used by the colleges.

Education and the Social Mobility of Minority Groups

A special case of the importance of education and social mobility is that of minorities, who are coming to higher education in larger numbers just as the problem of oversupply is becoming acute. Less than a decade has passed since the higher education community began an intense effort to open access for minorities to the whole range of colleges and universities. In that time, the nature of the problem has shifted from discrimination in admissions to a more complex set of issues.

From what little evidence is available, the relationship between higher education and mobility for minorities seems more direct than for white students (perhaps as a result, minority students place a higher value on gaining a post-secondary education than do their white counterparts).[33] To succeed without such credentials is difficult for whites, but almost impossible for minorities, so that the trend for credentials to be necessary but not sufficient is even more true for minority applicants. As the Supreme Court noted in the Griggs vs. Duke Power Case, the arbitrary use of credentials for screening applicants often works against minority applicants.[34]

Self-confidence and self-esteem are critical problems, particularly in terms of one's perception of career opportunities, and these seem to be altered by participation in postsecondary education. Whereas the ability of college degrees to insure entrance to the middle class is eroding as degrees proliferate, they still have a more powerful ability to certify middle-class membership for minorities than for whites.

In terms of minority access to higher education, the progress so far is undeniable. The *Report on Higher Education,* using the figures for blacks as an indicator of minority access, noted that the number of blacks as a percentage of all students began to rise in 1967.[35] Since the completion of that report, the progress with regard to access has been even more marked.[36] In the year 1970–1971, for example, total enrollment increased by about 4%, but black enrollment increased by 17%. In measuring this progress, it is important to note that the percentage of black students was *declining* in the period immediately before 1967.[37]

At the time of the *Report* the data on other minorities— Chicanos, Puerto Ricans, and native Americans—were so skimpy as to make evaluation of their enrollments difficult. Since that time, more evidence has become available and it is clear that the number of students within these groups, as percentages of all students, is also rising steadily. In 1970–1971, the enrollment of Spanish-speaking students rose 19%.[38]

Although the data are less adequate for graduate schools, in the last few years the share of minority graduate students has also begun to rise. In 1970–1971, black graduate enrollment rose 38% and that of Spanish-speaking students rose 31%. However, the share of minority students as a percentage of all graduate students is still far below, something less than half, that at the undergraduate level, and still far below the minority share of the age cohort.[39]

Table 2. Non-White Career Participation: A Measure of Change since 1960

		Non-White	White
Professional and technical workers	1960	4.8	12.1
(percent of each work force)	1972	9.5	14.6
Percent of each work force	1960	10.2	4.9
unemployed	1972	10.0	5.0
Percent of families with income of	1960	13.3	35.9
$10,000 or more (adjusted for price	1972	33.7	59.2
changes in 1972 constant dollars)			
Median Income of Families	1960	$4,564	$ 8,267
	1972	$7,106	$11,549

Source: *New York Times*, August 26, 1973.

But even more important, as Table 2 shows, the new Census data indicate that more and more college-educated young people from minority communities are moving steadily into jobs (and income ranges) consistent with a pattern of upward mobility.[40]

Given this progress, many educators see the present needs of minority education primarily in financial terms. While resources are essential, it is important to take into account the growing split between those minority students who are "making it" in postsecondary education and in later careers, and those who are not.[41] For this latter group, the basic instincts of the traditional campus are wrong, and they are even less likely to gain from access than are the white students who aren't "making it" in higher education. In this sense, the problems of minority students are less discrimination in admission or even adequate financial support and are closer to the problems of all students. The question is increasingly the same: How can effective opportunities be created for those students not well served by the current institutions?

However, there remain a number of problems peculiar to minorities. Among those minority students not "making it," there are many who lack motivation and self-esteem and more whose world is a subculture alienated from the mainstream of society (as described in several recent studies)[42] so that their lives are outside any foreseeable role in the post-secondary education community. This is particularly the case for native Americans as well as for some urban blacks, Chicanos, and Puerto Ricans.

Minorities are still disproportionately entering the least selective institutions. As Table 3 shows, bright male minority students are more than twice as likely to enter a community college and less than two-thirds as likely to enter a university as their white counterparts.

Just as minority students have arrived at the graduate school doors, the pressure for admission from white males and newly liberated women searching for a suitable credential is mounting. Consequently, new resistance to minority progress in graduate school admissions is appearing.[43]

Programs of support for minority students have been harder to create at the graduate than at the undergraduate level. Not only are almost all federal (and many state) graduate fellowship programs declining, but student aid at the graduate level is also more complicated. Because there is an assumed rough correlation between the terms "minority" and "low-income" at the undergraduate level, there is public acceptance for a significant proportion of student aid going to minority students; and the general programs of aid

Table 3. Distribution of Male Students Among Types of Institutions, by High School Grade Averages, 1970

Average high school grade	Percent enrolled in two-year colleges		Percent enrolled in four-year colleges				Percent enrolled in universities	
			Predominantly white		Predominantly black			
	Blacks	Whites	Blacks	Whites	Blacks	Whites	Blacks	Whites
A or A+	10%	4%	12%	40%	46%	.09%	33%	56%
B+	24	12	25	43	24	.13	27	44
B	16	24	19	40	44	.18	19	36
C+	28	44	18	33	41	.28	14	23
C	42	59	16	26	34	.29	8	16
D	54	66	21	21	21	.47	5	14

Note: Columns may not add up to 100 percent because of rounding.
Source: *Toward Equal Opportunity for Higher Education*, p. 44.

to low-income students do reach most minority students.[44] That correlation is far less clear at the graduate level. There are no general programs of aid specifically targeted for low-income graduate students. On what grounds can student aid be targeted for minority students? What role should family income play when determining financial need for graduate students? [45]

A significant share of all minority students attend the predominantly black colleges and the few Spanish-speaking and native American ethnic colleges; yet the very success of opening access to the predominantly white colleges threatens the viability of these institutions. After years of important

service on starvation budgets, their influence, now that minority education is finally front and center, has diminished
as many of the best minority students and brightest young
faculty are attracted to predominantly white institutions.[46]

But, increasingly, the critical problem for minority students is merging with the critical problem of white students
—encouraging the development of institutions of postsecondary education which are effective in meeting the needs
of diverse students, particularly those who do not learn well
in the conventional academic format.

Resources are needed. At the graduate level, we believe a
program of national fellowships, as described in our position
paper on graduate education, will help, among others, talented minority students.[47] With regard to the black and
ethnic colleges, public and private, there is an obvious current need for federal support. Yet it is not logical for the
federal government to subsidize these institutions permanently. Present funding should be designed so as to be an
incentive to help such institutions achieve a viable and
competitive role in higher education without special federal
assistance. Too often general institutional aid simply becomes a subsidy for continued operation, postponing the
interest in institutional reform. Their futures should depend
on the enhancement of their intrinsic values.

There are a few disturbing signs of a flagging of the commitment to minority opportunity within postsecondary education.[48] Much of the intensity of this commitment in the
late 1960s came from a national sense of guilt and fear. Today, both of those emotions are much diminished. We believe that it is important for this country to recommit itself
to educational opportunities for minorities based neither on

fear nor on guilt, but on a determined interest in social equity.[49]

Strategies in an Era of Underemployment
In light of the oversupply, or underemployment, of college graduates, major shifts in educational policies have been put forward, including:

Deliberate cutbacks in college attendance. (We disagree. A college education can make a contribution both to the individual and society beyond its value as a preparation for a specific career. Broader access, so long sought, is changing the aspirations and opportunities of the less advantaged, creating a more open and mobile society.

We believe that where specialized education is mandatory and access necessarily limited, standards for admission should more clearly represent societal needs. But in general, a more equitable—and effective—approach will be to provide access to education and let the competition for the best career opportunities occur on the job, rather than at the admissions door.)

Shifting primary emphasis to vocational and career training. (Such training should be accorded greater legitimacy, but it should not be seen as a substitute for liberal arts, which has its own broader values. Students should be able to take either or both, *in whatever order* meets their needs.)

Detailed and comprehensive state or federal manpower planning. (Considering the notable lack of success of governmental agencies to date—planning, for example, for a teacher shortage while the problem of oversupply was already upon us[50]—such an approach would be both inhibiting to freedom and openness and most likely unsuccessful.)

Education is not rigidly tracked in this country, as it is in Europe, so that graduates here are able to move to less-crowded careers. Also, there is no tradition in this country, as in India or the Philippines, that most jobs are beneath the dignity of the educated, so that there is no accumulation here of frustrated and unemployed college-trained individuals.[51] On the contrary, Americans show great flexibility in adapting to changing employment opportunities.

This is not to say that no broad planning should be attempted. The federal government can help by developing and disseminating more reliable data on the supply and demand for highly-educated manpower. In areas of obvious shortage, federal incentives can help encourage expansion. For example, this country trains approximately 9,000 physicians per year, but imports another 10,000 from abroad. Adding insult to injury, 600 Americans annually go abroad to study at foreign medical schools.[52] Yet, in this field, the federal government proposed elimination of support for students only one year after establishing strong federal incentives for the expansion of health education enrollment.[53]

Under any foreseeable conditions, there will be substantial underemployment of college graduates in relation to the traditional view of "college-type" jobs. A more rational relationship between education and careers can come about if realistic opportunities exist for students to return to formal education on a recurrent basis throughout life, as noted in the next chapter. This would allow the starting of a career without the feeling that one has lost one's only opportunity to insure social mobility through education, would allow an initial career choice without the fear that one has made an irrevocable life commitment, and would also allow a weighing of the value of varying types of education. There will always be competition for the "best" career opportunities, but wherever possible it should be based on performance on the job rather than in the classroom.

We believe that colleges and universities must turn toward a more honest presentation of their role and value in society. In the past, the higher education community has argued eloquently for the broad value to society and the student of a sound general education. But behind that rhetorical front there has been a quiet argument for a second value—that of a college credential as a guarantee of a good job, high income, and social status. In asking the support of society, we believe that colleges must stand less on their value as certifying agencies, and more on their value as educating agencies.

The fundamental values of a general education have been put forward as the useful preparation of the individual for a productive life, for social responsibility, and for personal fulfillment. But if these values are to be the yardstick, then it is essential to insure that academic programs do indeed provide an education that is effective for these purposes. A reexamination and renewal of all of postsecondary education and particularly of liberal education may therefore be the most important agenda item of the 1970s.

3
New Requirements
for Effective Education

Now that millions are entering postsecondary education with a wide range of skills and diverse goals, it can no longer be assumed that all, or even most, students will be qualified for or motivated by conventional academic instruction, nor that most will be well served by the traditional assumptions about the appropriate time and place for higher education. The following points will serve as a focus of our discussion of effective education:

For any serious learning to take place, the student must be motivated to take advantage of what college can provide, yet there are few perceived alternatives to college and few if any barriers to prevent the unmotivated student from drifting or dropping out.

Access, to be useful, must be to an educational opportunity appropriate for the student, and this requires a diversity of institutions beyond that available today.

The need and readiness for formal learning will occur at differing and multiple times in the lives of individuals, requiring recurrent educational opportunities.

The Need for Motivated Learning

In earlier educational eras the motivation of the student was not an issue of public policy. When higher education served an aristocracy, college attendance was a class-conferred privilege, which, if not taken seriously, was of no apparent cost to society. With the advent of meritocratic rules, students who were able at the academic arts earned the right to attend, and administrators and faculty assumed that the student would seek to make good use of his hard-won right. Attrition occurred and not all students were serious, but this was still seen as the student's loss and not society's. College was for the elite and those who wasted an opportunity available only to the select few could be dismissed as foolish.[1]

Today, as a result of the long and successful effort to make access easy, the question of a student's motivation cannot be so readily ignored. As the barriers of income and academic selectivity have fallen and as the use of college credentials as job prerequisites has proliferated, a majority of today's youth see college attendance as merely obligatory. Often, serious motivation to learn in college is lacking.[2]

As a rough generalization, there are two groups for whom motivation is a problem. One consists of students generally in the lower third of high school graduates. Pressured by parents, counselors, peers, and the need for credentials, they enter college. These "new learners" are not without ability and motivation, but often their abilities are clearly not academic, nor are they necessarily motivated to pursue a style of learning which many of them have already found frustrating in high school.[3] They may be strongly motivated to learn applied skills, or to learn from experience rather than from abstractions. Certainly they are usually motivated by a desire for credentials.[4] They may be willing to commit themselves if they find a college experience which builds on their talents; and institutions organized to do this, such as the College for Human Services or Alabama A&M, have demonstrated that attrition among nonacademic learners can be sharply reduced.[5] Or, as the experience of Vietnam veterans and older students indicates, if they are allowed to enter college a few years later in life, they are more likely to be motivated to learn even from traditional academic programs.[6]

The second group consists of those academically talented students who drift purposelessly through higher education. Despite their lack of interest, many attend college because they have been "trained for the contest since birth" [7] or because they fail to perceive an alternative. The very lack of barriers to entrance tends to diminish the student's sense of purpose. Some drift in and out of college repeatedly, never engaging themselves either in the process of study on the campus nor in any serious career or volunteer enterprise off campus, oblivious to the enormous costs to themselves and society entailed by spending unmotivated time in college.[8]

Conscious student choice is essential to motivation. By this we do not mean that students need to design their own programs of education. Rather, we mean that a student needs to be able to make a reasoned choice among clearly different options to pursue a particular style of learning at a particular time and place. For some, such a conscious choice will result in the student leaving college until he is clear as to his interests, for others it will mean the opportunity to choose an educational program that builds on the student's interests and talents.

Restructuring admissions or student aid programs to encourage motivated learning is not simple, since motivation is not readily measured. Self-confidence and a sense of purpose are central, yet these are often hampered by any barriers to access which seem arbitrary. For many students, broader personal and work experience before, between, or even during the college years is essential for more motivated learning.[9]

It is ironic that the educational community has accepted so fully the value of the period away from schooling that has occurred in the case of returning GIs. After an initial period of hostility to the concept of the GI Bill when it was proposed, educators have generally come to assume that considerable benefits to both students and the educational community have resulted. But they have never acted upon this example or attempted to broaden the use of the concept —despite a number of studies which show that, on the whole, those who left the educational lockstep and returned after their military service usually obtained higher grades, enjoyed the college experience more, were appreciated more by the faculty, and were more motivated, if for no other reason than because they had made a conscious choice to enter or reenter college.[10] Similar results have been found in studies of returning Peace Corps veterans, of women returning to Sarah Lawrence after their child-bearing years, and of older students entering the University of Texas.[11] The campus has much to gain from age diversity, for older students bring the benefits of their own experience to many others through peer influence in college.[12] It would seem reasonable, therefore, to extend the concept of spending periods away from schooling more widely in American post-secondary education.

Federal programs can encourage and legitimize such external experience by expanding student aid based on work-study and cooperative approaches, by expanding federal volunteer programs that extend the alternatives open to the young, by revising federal student aid to make it more available to older students, and by adapting the concept, so successful in the GI Bill, of providing educational benefits for those who have served their country and extending it to include community service, not just military service.[13]

The Need for Diversity
Student motivation is in part a function of *when* the student is in college, but is also a function of *what type of col-*

lege the student attends. To this end, a greater diversity is essential to accommodate the new and far broader range of abilities and interests of entering students.

The response on the part of many educators to such a proposition is, "But we are diverse! We have public and private institutions. We have two-year colleges, four-year colleges, and graduate schools. We have liberal arts, vocational, and career education and we have large and small institutions."

Though true, this misses the point, for the real issue is whether the nature and extent of diversity matches the needs of the students seeking an education. What is the range of choice from the vantage point of those who want to develop differing skills, who want to capitalize on differing abilities, or who learn in different ways? In these respects, the range of diversity in American education is too limited.[14] We believe that to increase the effectiveness of teaching and learning, there must be incentives for each institution to sharpen the focus of its mission and to rethink its approach to teaching and learning.

Nearly all of today's colleges and universities see it as their mission to impart knowledge organized primarily in terms of academic disciplines: of history and political science, chemistry and biology, sociology and psychology. Most feel no learning is legitimate that fails to fit into a standard academic box. To be diverse (or, in the accepted term, "comprehensive") within an institution is to cover a wide range of such disciplines. Yet there is no logical reason to assume that the mission of education is to force students into common patterns of academic achievement differing only in level of accomplishment. For some students, the comprehensive, discipline-based college or university is appropriate;

most, however, learn more effectively in institutions of different but focused missions.[15]

The classroom lecture has been the dominant educational method, just as the academic disciplines have been the dominant approach to organization. Many colleges are now exploring alternatives to the classroom lecture format,[16] but across the landscape of American higher education, learning is still largely a spectator sport. The fact that American higher education has institutionalized a single system involving academic years, in which knowledge is fragmented into courses, attended at fixed times and in which teachers and students play prescribed and routinized roles, helps explain the lack of diversity. The four-year curriculum, almost universally copied from an arbitrary and ancient decision at Harvard, stays firmly fixed despite widespread recognition that many students need a longer period of college and some a much shorter time.[17]

Fortunately, there is a new interest in diversity. A variety of new postsecondary institutions have been organized: open universities, single-purpose institutions, experimental subcolleges, ethnic colleges, urban learning centers, cooperative programs, off-campus internships, and many others. But the number of students in such programs remains small compared to total enrollments in postsecondary education.

Variations in the sequences, times, pace, and intensities of learning can come about through changes in governance, decentralization, and moves to new physical settings. Often such changes are the means by which teachers and students can be encouraged to reconsider why they are doing what they are doing. Other educating agencies in American society—the Armed Services, language schools and schools of performing arts, research corporations, businesses, clinical hospitals, planning organizations, and a host of other agencies—provide models of the enormous variety of ways individuals can be organized to teach and to learn.[18]

There are several strategies that we believe are workable in encouraging diversity. First, it is desirable to encourage the development of new institutions. This is not because *more* institutions are needed but because one important avenue to imaginative and diverse institutions is entrepreneurial experimentation. A harsh but necessary concomitant is that there must also be room for the demise of ineffective institutions as well, both public and private.

Second, society should recognize and legitimize the serious educational activities of peripheral institutions, including those of the Armed Services, proprietary institutions, and industry. These segments of postsecondary education probably meet the needs of adults in a more comprehensive way than any other.

Third, it is desirable to preserve the conditions under which a healthy and effective private sector of postsecondary education can continue. The issue is not whether private higher education is more effective or more diverse than public. The combination of public and private *is* more effective and more diverse than public alone. More important than ever is the point that the relative independence of some institutions helps insure the vitality and freedom of all.

We believe that the national interest can best be served by a varied system which includes institutions offering programs of differing length and learning style in differing social settings, public and private, nonprofit and proprietary, all competing under conditions which encourage each institution to pay healthy attention to its own effectiveness.

In moving in these directions, educational standards can

and should be raised, not lowered. Commitment to innovation and diversity should not be an excuse for a lack of structure or a failure to demand performance on the part of the student.

Recurrent Education

Until very recently, the public has tended to see postsecondary education as a launching pad. The nature and length of the educational experience determines the career and life orbit the student will enter—an orbit in which we expect him to remain throughout his life. There is now a growing awareness in American society that formal education is not something that must be completed in one block prior to any career experience.

There are a number of reasons for the gradual erosion of this concept and an interest in "recurrent education"—a term first used in Europe.[19] One of the most frequently put forward is the problem of educational obsolescence. Not only must a physician or engineer periodically take the time to upgrade his technical knowledge, but there is today a general perception that the entire work force must be more flexible. As jobs change at all levels, education can be useful in minimizing the limitations of manpower planning and the inflexibility of the labor market.[20]

There are three other reasons that are perhaps more significant. First, there is the desirability of providing many people an opportunity to start new careers. Some will find it useful to return for more education to help them move upward along a career ladder. (This is one of the main concerns in Europe—providing an equitable opportunity for older students who did not have the opportunity for college or university work when they turned eighteen.) Others, probably a growing number, will want the opportunity for lateral movement (for example, the businessman who in middle age seeks some new challenge to tackle and wishes to begin studying for a degree in education).

The second reason is that a recurrent pattern matches the requirements of *most* students better than the traditional pattern. Most, as noted above, are trapped too long in the academic lockstep, isolated from careers and unsure of their own interests.

Third, for many persons already well into careers, a recurrent educational opportunity would allow a period of personal reorganization. College is a period of suspension, both in terms of personal development and career—a period when one can think of goals without the social pressure to be "doing something." Our society seems to be moving toward a time when such periods of suspension and reexamination will be appropriate on more than one occasion. For such recurrent students, the new period of development and reaffirmation can do much to keep alive a sense of excitement in their lives. Also, the benefits of a reaffirmation of purpose and a return to study go beyond those accrued by the student; a recent study has indicated that children of parents involved in recurrent education patterns also benefit.[21]

Change is necessary to create more open and available recurrent education. Some changes on the job are necessary as well. There is a need for career ladders, on which one can move one rung at a time. Can, for example, a talented and motivated computer programmer become a computer engineer and ultimately a computer scientist? Can a nurse become a doctor? [22]

There already exist a number of traditional avenues by which students past the normal college age may gain further education. They include:

University extension programs.

High school adult education programs.

University-level correspondence schools (as in the oldest and best-known at Oklahoma University).

Television colleges (as at the Chicago Community College of the Air, the State University of Nebraska, and Coast College or Cañada College in California).

A variety of programs run by volunteer organizations, such as the YMCA.

Internal training programs run by industry.

And, of course, one should not forget the growing number of students beyond the normal college age who enroll at traditional campuses.

But, despite the variety, there are problems of legitimacy, standards, and effectiveness. Within the academic world these programs tend to be treated as second-class. More often than not they are unable to offer degrees. Frequently, extension courses are not accepted for credit for an on-campus degree even by their parent organization. Legislatures provide less funding per student than for traditional, full-time, daytime programs. Many student aid programs either do not allow enrollment in such programs or have serious restrictions. Accrediting regulations often hamper acceptance. The implication is that what is learned in a 9 A.M. class by a full-time student is more significant than what is learned in an 8 P.M. class by a part-time student.[23]

In many such programs, the physical setting of the learning process is important. Many students beyond the normal college age find the campus uncongenial, designed and run only for young people. Frequently, because recurrent programs are often simply reduced versions of the conventional academic program on campus, a sense of participation is missing and there is lack of peer interaction. Only recently, as the Open Universities or the Universities Without Walls around the country have been developed, has there been a serious attempt to create new peer interaction forms for off-campus students.[24] One useful aspect of these developments has been the tendency to restore the student rather than the curriculum to the center of the learning process.

Recurrent education also calls for a new form of what we currently call counseling—making available information by which students can make decisions. Recurrent education implies that students will be better equipped to decide among their educational options, yet many will have less access to the conventional sources of information. Obviously the high school counselor will be neither available nor appropriate for this group. College counseling offices usually have information only on that one institution's own programs. It is likely, therefore, that new vehicles must be found to make information more readily available.[25]

There are other difficult issues besides the availability of information. The most motivated students (who are often already the best educated) will want to go back to postsecondary education several times. On what basis should federal support be available? Should it be on the basis of a certain number of months of eligibility (such as the GI Bill provides)? Or if it is to be available on the basis of merit, will it favor those most in need of recurrent opportunities?

What distinctions should be made between going back in order to study for a new career and going back to study only for one's own enjoyment? Should public resources allow anyone to study anything, or just those subjects that lend themselves to specific tasks? Is there an upper age limit past which society should have no interest or obligation to provide support? Should student aid take into account the greater needs of a student who at a later point in his life has already developed family responsibilities and has become accustomed to a higher level of income?

For a number of years, both the French and Germans have had established programs of support for recurrent education. In both cases, there are government programs of employee benefits that result in something like a faculty sabbatical.[26] Similar plans have been suggested to support recurrent education patterns in this country (the federal government already provides a program for certain of its employees, as do a few companies). Some proposals that have been suggested for funding recurrent students include the use of employees' benefits, variations of the Social Security program, a special version of unemployment insurance, or even government-insured mortgages on homes.[27]

There are, in short, a host of questions with regard to the possibility, nature, and extent of federal support for individuals who opt for recurrent patterns of education which will in the future require detailed research and careful analysis.

We believe the federal government can do much to encourage motivated learning, recurrent education, and diverse institutions by expanding support of work-study and cooperative education, by supporting and legitimizing alternatives to schooling (particularly alternatives involving public service), by revising student aid guidelines to accommodate a broader student age range, by beginning serious study of methods for supporting students returning later in life, by learning to deal with a wider range of postsecondary institutions, and by encouraging more effective competition among the institutions of postsecondary education.

But in encouraging these concepts, federal programs must contend with powerful new political realities in the educational community—a new inertia within colleges and universities that accompanies the end of a long period of growth, entanglement in the restrictions of professionalism, and a revolution in the organization of educational decision-making.

4
New Political Realities

For effective federal action, a range of new political realities must be taken into account.

The political landscape of American higher education is changing dramatically. With the end of two and a half decades of dynamic growth, new rigidities which were submerged or inhibited by growth are appearing in the body politic of many institutions. At the same time, an organizational revolution is rapidly shifting key educational decision-making from the college campuses to the headquarters of large multicampus systems, the coordinating agencies and superboards of state government, faculty unions, and the state and federal courts. Professional groups of various kinds, acting through state governments and in national alliances, continue to develop new rules of accreditation, certification, and licensure affecting the freedom of movement of individuals and institutions.

The End of Dynamic Growth
Most higher education institutions are now organizationally middle-aged. In the last twenty-five years of unparalleled growth, the average campus size has doubled. Huge campuses have developed. Approximately a third of all students in higher education now attend campuses with enrollments of more than 20,000.[1]

At increasing numbers of campuses, 70% or more of the faculty is tenured, and the slowdown of enrollment increases makes it more and more difficult to introduce new blood. A decade ago, the average age of faculties was dropping. Now, with fewer and fewer openings, it is rising and almost 60% are 40 or older.[2]

The rigidities of middle age are exacerbated by the new demographic and economic prospects confronting higher education. Large yearly increases in enrollment are now a thing of the past. The 1973 fall enrollment was up only 2%, compared to an average 8% yearly increase in the 1960s.[3] Large and automatic funding increases are much less likely. Federal funding, for example, increased only 42% over the last five years, compared with 182% in the five years preceding these.[4] Further expansion of higher education will be restrained at best.

All this means that change in higher education will have to take place under conditions very different from those which existed in the 1960s. Not all the new forces favor the status quo. To some extent, the perils and pressures facing higher education have brought a sense of urgency into the competition for students and resources and have created positive concern for the effectiveness of educational programs. As long as there were always greater numbers of students clamoring for admission and easy sources of new funding available, there was little perception of and patience with the need for the wrenching process of analysis and self-improvement. But change must now come about not simply as an additive process, but through the more difficult process of reallocating existing resources from old programs to new ideas.

Since opportunities for recruitment of new faculty will be limited, the means must be developed to create new interests and new skills among existing faculty. Reform and change through institutional self-renewal should be the order of the day.

The Revolution in Decision-Making
Most of the public, and many people on campus, still perceive higher education as consisting of a number of colleges

and universities, some public, some private, each independent of the others and each physically embodied on a defined campus. The college or university president is seen as *the* significant administrative officer, acting in his role as the titular head of the faculty and responsible with his staff for not only such academic concerns as admissions policies, but such financial concerns as obtaining the necessary resources from the alumni or the legislature. For better or worse, this concept is almost as outdated as thinking of a single school in a large urban elementary and secondary system, such as that of New York or Detroit, as a center of educational policy with the principal as the all-powerful administrator.

One critical factor in this revolution, dating back only to 1950, is the decline of the private sector in higher education. For the first fifty years of this century, enrollment was evenly split—half public and half private. Both sectors grew slowly and at the same rate. But with the huge growth rates of the 1950s and 1960s, private resources were simply not adequate to continue comparable growth rates. From 1950–1967, both public and private enrollments were growing, as Figure 1 shows, but the public sector was growing much more rapidly. Starting in 1968, private enrollment leveled off and during the last year or two it has decreased until today enrollment in higher education is 76% public and 24% private.[5] In some major states the ratio is even greater, as in California where it is 90% and 10%, and in a few states public institutions represent essentially all of higher education.[6]

The warning signs of crisis have been repeatedly announced. There has been a small but growing attrition of smaller colleges, the latest casualties being a 77-year-old junior college in Massachusetts and a 4-year-old black sep-

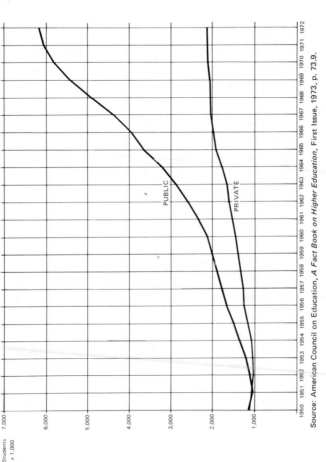

Source: American Council on Education, *A Fact Book on Higher Education*, First Issue, 1973., p. 73.9.

Figure 1. Enrollment in Institutions of Higher Education by Type of Institution Control, 1950–1972.

aratist college in North Carolina.[7] A number of well-known private universities, including Houston, Buffalo, Vermont, Temple, and Pittsburgh, have become public or quasipublic institutions, as have a number of less well-known colleges. There has been a new trend toward merger as well.[8] But only recently has the threat to the viability and the influence of private higher education become serious, particularly in the ever-increasing gap between public and private cost to the student (see Figure 2).[9]

A parallel development has been a decline in the local control of municipal and community institutions. There have always been a modest number of city-supported universities such as City University of New York or the University of Cincinnati. Similarly, the community college was usually established through a local taxing district and governed by a local board. Today both types of institutions are becoming steadily more dependent on state resources, and in one case after another are being absorbed into state systems.

A powerful new trend is the shift in organization of the public sector. In state after state, public campuses have been organized into major multicampus systems which now incorporate over three-quarters of the students attending state universities and colleges and a growing share of community college students. In some cases these started with a single university campus which in turn established branches (as at the Universities of Texas, Illinois, and North Carolina). In other cases, disparate colleges, often small teachers' colleges, mining schools, and the like, were brought together and rebuilt into much larger state colleges and then supplemented by new campuses (as in the State University of New York, or in the California State Colleges and Universities).[10]

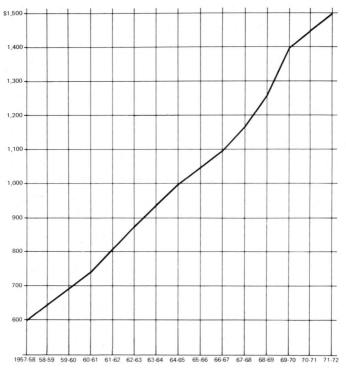

Source: U.S. Office of Education, *Basic Student Charges,* U.S. Government Printing Office.

Figure 2. Tuition Gap Between Public and Private Institutions.

Many states have developed more than one multicampus system, based sometimes on geography (as in New York), sometimes on educational function (as in California), and sometimes mainly on traditional or historic rationales (as in Illinois). As each system competes for resources, their large and ever more politically skilled bureaucracies begin to vie with one another.[11] One result has been that legisla-

tures and governors have found an inevitable need for some
agency to control and coordinate the systems themselves, ac-
celerating the trend to creating coordinating bodies and
superboards as well as the trend to increasing the powers
of these agencies. Table 1 shows that evolution.

There are both advantages and disadvantages to these
two potent and pervasive changes. Given the growth in the
numbers of students, the number of institutions, and the
size of budgets, some system of organization and management of institutions is required. It is manifestly impossible
for a legislature to supervise the operation of 30 or 50 or
100 campuses. The use of the multicampus system concept
is thus a logical outcome of growth.

At the same time, there is a need for coordination, for
an agency that represents students and the general public
in statewide planning, for an institutionally independent
but knowledgeable source of information for the legislature

Table 1. Changes in Form of State Coordination from 1939–1969

States with:	1939*	1949*	1959	1964	1969
No formal coordination	33	28	17	11	3
Voluntary coordination	0	3	7	4	1
Coordination boards	2	3	10	18	27
Advisory	(1)	(1)	(5)	(11)	(13)
Regulatory	(1)	(2)	(5)	(7)	(14)
Consolidated governing board	15	16	16	17	19

* Including the territories of Alaska and Hawaii.
Source: Adapted by Robert Berdahl, *Statewide Coordination of Higher
Education*, American Council on Education, Washington, D.C., 1971,
p. 35.

and governor. If coordinating agencies were not in place today, they would no doubt be invented.

Both types of agencies have made important contributions
to the evolution of postsecondary education. Managerial
posts in both are increasingly filled with capable administrators whose roles provide them with a broad perspective of
the educational needs within their states. In a number of
states they have addressed current problems with imagination and courage, sometimes becoming a major force for
enhancing institutional diversity. One need only think of
the experiments in open universities in New York and Minnesota, the nontraditional campuses in Washington or
Wisconsin, the upper-division colleges in Illinois or Florida,
the experiments with subcolleges in Alabama or California,
as well as many more.

As they themselves are quick to recognize, however, these
managers are ever further removed from regular contact
with students and faculty. And, particularly in the case of
officers of multicampus systems, they are constantly restrained by the need to be the advocate for their institutional constituencies.[12]

Within multicampus systems, with the increasing concern
for accountability, there is an almost inexorable pressure
for decisions to gravitate upward in the organization, off
campus, into the home office. Often the result is that the
system usurps prerogatives that were once exercised at the
campus level, including admissions policies, financial decisions, policies with regard to faculty hiring practices and
workloads, building priorities and architectural planning,
control over new programs, and many others.[13]

Coordinating agencies have historically been frustrated by
their inability to influence the course of the institutions

they are supposed to be coordinating, particularly in the case of prestigious state universities. The result has been a determined effort on the part of such agencies (often at the behest of the governor or legislature) to wrest power from the multicampus systems. In the process, they have tended to slip away from the planning and coordinating role and become instead another organizational layer between the campus and the capitol, devoted to the problems of institutional management.

The danger lies in the tendency for these two types of agencies, with size and age, to become more and more bureaucratic. Similarity becomes easier to deal with than diversity. Administrators are chosen more for their skill and reputation for offending no one than for their imaginative leadership. Concern for creating an effective education matching the differing needs of students gives way to concern for the appearance of meeting directives from above. And the percentage of resources devoted to administration rises steadily.

The courts, which have historically left the educational community to regulate itself, are now being drawn into a role as decision makers, expanding their interests in the area of postsecondary education as they have everywhere in this age of litigation. New case law ranges over the right of the campus to determine admissions policies, faculty hiring and firing, student discipline, accrediting procedures, and the relevance of academic credentials in selecting an employee. In one area of academic administration after another, the potential for legal action has begun to alter the reality of decision-making.

Just as the trend toward campuses' losing their prerogatives as the ultimate decision makers was becoming most

pronounced, in many states public employees were gaining
the right to organize and the federal National Labor Relations Act guidelines were being modified to allow the organization of employees of any sizable college or university
—and, as a result, faculty unions have been organized in
increasing numbers. Often, where there is a systemwide
centralization, the frustration of faculties in their attempts
to resolve issues with the various campus administrations
leads them to attempt to create systemwide faculty unions
with the power necessary to match that of the multicampus
administration.[14] By November of 1972, 121 four-year institutions and 147 two-year institutions, all but a few publicly
supported, had faculty unions, the most aggressive being
those at public campuses which are parts of major systems.[15]
Whatever its benefits, the result of unionization is usually
the creation of a whole new bureaucracy, and once again
educational issues are lost from view in the resulting reorganization of prerogatives and power.[16]

As a result of this organizational revolution, the relationships among the key actors in both the state and federal
arenas of educational politics are being permanently altered.
Basic political issues—who gets what and who decides what
—are being resolved on new terms, and options once considered normal are now being foreclosed.

Within the state arena, the shifting relationships between
individual campuses and central authorities (and now often
unions as well) are imposing change. The escalation of interest in accountability means more emphasis on budgets and
program approvals as vehicles for control, and new efforts
at regulating campus life through measures such as faculty
work rules.[17] The competition between public and private

institutions is affected as the superboards move to extend their control to private institutions.

In the national arena, federal programs must contend with unfamiliar forces. New and effective power brokers from state systems argue for state agency clearance of projects and for a larger voice in the making of federal policy. In this new political setting, there is pressure to erode the historic federal practice of direct relationships with individual students and individual campuses and the even-handed treatment of public and private institutions.[18]

We believe there must be careful analysis of the evolving organizational structure of higher education by both federal and state policy makers. The federal government has often, without such analysis, deepened the problems noted above by requiring the creation of state agencies or functions for its own bureaucratic convenience. We believe state officials, particularly those in statewide coordinating boards and the offices of multicampus systems, should give high priority to the creation of effective means for achieving their objectives through incentives that allow decentralized management of the educational process in a conscious reversal of the current trend. Both types of agencies need real power for the exercise of their responsibilities. Incentives powerful enough to alter traditional faculty and campus behavior are required in order that education within each state can be responsive to the public need.

We believe the federal government can assist in the reversal of this trend toward centralization of educational decision-making by reviewing its demands on states for centralized agencies, by recognizing the differences between multicampus systems and coordinating boards, by helping these agencies strengthen the incentives for campus and faculty responsiveness, and by increasing emphasis on direct funding of students in order to maximize their freedom of choice.

The Restraints of Professionalism

Professionalism in our society is increasing and the concept of the professional credential is being applied over an ever wider part of the spectrum of careers. At one point, credentialized professionals included doctors, lawyers, and the clergy, then architects and engineers, then psychologists and teachers, and now morticians and dancing school instructors. Almost all occupational groups gravitate relentlessly toward becoming licensed and restricted professions.[19] Essential to this has been a defining, through accreditation, certification, and licensure, of the educational requirements for entry to the profession. Group self-interest is not perforce unhealthy. But the rush toward professionalization—particularly in the last three decades—has often been at the expense of equitable access to careers, consumer protection, and individual opportunity for advancement.

Licensing has become an occupational status symbol. In 1939 the Wisconsin legislature mandated that house painters must take examinations and be licensed. A person caught painting without a license could be arrested and fined. The State Supreme Court found the law unconstitutional. In 1955 a bill was introduced in California which would have required the licensing of grass-cutters as "maintenance gardeners." The bill included provisions for a state board to administer the profession to prevent "gross incompetence, negligence and misrepresentation." Violators could have been punished by a fine of up to $500 and up to six months in jail.[20] This particular bill did not pass, but hundreds have. Such laws are sought not only to provide for the regulation of entry into the field, but to provide the group in question with a primary role as the regulators. About half of the occupational licensing laws in the states require that all members of the licensing board be licensed practitioners.[21] Where not specifically provided, professional associations are usually "consulted." So the CPAs sit on the State Board of Public Accountants, and the architects license future architects, all in the name of the state.

If the standards used by examining and licensing boards were reasonably related to the demands of the occupation, the self-serving nature of the process might be tolerable. However, the standards employed often bear only a tenuous relationship to the competencies needed for successful practice, and instead often reflect more the profession's image of itself.

In similar fashion, emerging professional groups seek to gain control over the training of new members through the process of accreditation. Since the American Medical Association's publication of a list of approved schools in 1906, practically every occupational and professional group has sought to approve educational programs in their respective fields.[22] Unlike regional accrediting associations, professional and occupational accrediting bodies are nationwide, and derive their power from the professional association. Consequently, they are responsive to the imperatives of the profession, not of the schools, their students, or the public. Because of the linkages with state licensing, educational institutions are in a weak position to argue with a professional accrediting group, since they might thus jeopardize their approved status and, as a result, bar their students from future careers. In some cases professions use accreditation as a means of restricting the number of entrants in an allied occupational field, as with the control exercised over medical technology education by pathologists.[23]

The standards utilized by professional accrediting groups have rarely been validated. Most have yet to demonstrate a relationship to later career success, nor have the standards employed been shown to correlate with even traditional indices of academic quality. Rather, standards in professional accrediting seem to be based on professional value judgments. Most frequently they concern indices of professional status, such as the number of Ph.D.'s on college faculties, library holdings, administrative structures, and so on.[24] (Thus the accrediting arm of the American Bar Association is generally acknowledged as having driven out most night law programs due to its insistence on full-time law school faculties.)

In order to cement their positions, professional and occupational groups seek tie-ins between state licensing and professional accreditation. Under the guise of protecting the public, licensing laws stipulate that one must graduate from a program accredited by the professional accrediting agency. Thus, just in order to sit for the bar exam, 39 states require graduation from a law school accredited by the American Bar Association, which, not coincidentally, also writes the exam, and evaluates the "moral fitness" of prospective members of the Bar.[25] Often members of the licensing boards are officers of the professional associations, or serve on the accrediting agencies as well. Thus, states have vested professions with legal sanction, reinforcing their power over individuals and virtually insuring the compliance of educational institutions.

As public funding of education has increased, federal and state governments have turned to professional accrediting agencies to determine the eligibility of educational institutions. The U.S. Commissioner of Education currently recognizes over 30 professional agencies which determine eligibility for federal programs.[26] By making eligibility for funds contingent on professional accreditation, further sanction is accorded professional groups. For an educational institution, losing professional accreditation may mean not only jeopardizing the opportunities of its graduates, but the loss of its public funding as well.

Society needs protection from fraudulent practitioners, and an assurance that individuals are competent to practice. Professional groups have legitimate interests in safeguarding public trust of the profession. Individuals have a right to be evaluated on the basis of their knowledge and competence, and to expect that such evaluation will be conducted under equitable conditions with valid measures. Yet too often licensing and professional accreditation develop into an entanglement of arbitrary rules and procedures which undermine individual opportunity, erode institutional flexibility, subordinate protection of the consumer, and give rise to major social inequities.

In an ever increasing number of fields, the delicate balance between considerations of quality and equality, individual rights and consumer protection has been lost.

With every passing year, our postsecondary education system becomes further entangled in laws for licensing, educational requirements for credentials, and more specialized procedures. Each year, the role of private, municipal, and community-controlled higher education diminishes. Each

year, the autonomy of the campus erodes as influence or
control over some further aspect of the educational process
moves toward a multicampus system headquarters, a governing board, a licensing agency, a faculty union, a state or
federal court, or a legislature. Each year, change in the system of education becomes more difficult. Now, while it is
still feasible, the federal government must consider how it
can assist in the encouragement of a more open and flexible
educational community.

5
The Federal Presence
in Higher Education

Today the federal government is deeply involved in post-secondary education, more so than is generally recognized. Not only is the federal government a major source of support, but it is also a major source of regulation. Its policies and programs in areas other than education have important, though often unintended, effects on the educational community. Despite being studied and restudied, federal policies for postsecondary education often fail to reflect the changes necessary because of the extent of federal involvement, the new role of state agencies, or the differing requirements of an egalitarian era.[1]

Federal aid to higher education began in the first year of the Constitution with grants of public lands for college endowments.[2] West Point, the first federal college, is over 170 years old. The Morrill or Land Grant College Act was passed more than 110 years ago. That act, with its emphasis on applied science and education for the nonelite, is a reminder of how powerful and how positive federal action can be.[3]

Federal interest in the support of colleges and universities can thus hardly be described as something new; but until World War II, federal involvement was modest and federal influence slight. An exception was the one-time impact of the endowment of the land-grant colleges. There were also precedents for federal aid in some of the programs of the New Deal, but these were seen less as antecedents and more as aberrations. As late as 1940, total federal funding was less than $50 million per year.[4] For most of the 1,600 colleges and universities of that time,[5] federal policy toward education was of little consequence.

With the start of the postwar period, all of this changed. By the end of the war, federal funding had reached $100 million annually. Two and a half decades later it had increased sixty-fold.[6] Over a dozen federal agencies besides the Office of Education now have extensive dealings with the institutions of postsecondary education, ranging from support of research in nuclear physics by the Atomic Energy Commission to support of occupational training by the Department of Labor. Altogether there are some 375 federal programs administered by 60 agencies that affect postsecondary education.[7] Federal regulations constrain both students and institutions. Federal policies in foreign or domestic affairs often inadvertently become policies in education.

After examining the broad range of the federal presence and the evolution of federal programs over the past twenty-five years, we have concluded that:

The federal intent to accomplish one goal often leads logically to a federal interest in other goals.

Programs intended to deal with a limited group of institutions tend to become diffused over time to cover a broader range of institutions.

Because of the decentralization of policy-making and the multiplicity of agencies, one federal initiative or regulation sometimes runs counter to another.

A sense of legitimacy for an issue of educational policy is often created by the existence of a federal program.

There has been a general trend toward a concern for equity.

Unintended effects are often as significant as the intended ones.

The federal government can, on occasion, end programs.

The Postwar Rationales for Federal Involvement

The growing involvement of the federal government in higher education flowed naturally out of the Second World War. The first federal interest was in the support of *re-*

search. Starting with a broadly accepted need to maintain a strong defense, it expanded with time to encompass the support of research for national concerns in atomic energy, space, health, education, poverty, and recently in the arts, the humanities, the environment, and energy.[8] As federal support broadened beyond an interest in defense, it also broadened beyond the need for new knowledge to include the need for trained manpower. For example, the need for new knowledge in high energy physics was extended to the need for physicists, and in turn to the need for greater numbers of college faculty teaching physics.

The second interest was *access*. The success of the GI Bill demonstrated the validity of college attendance by a far wider group than had originally been considered "college material." In turn, this led to a national interest in educational opportunity and to a whole range of student aid programs. Increasingly these programs focused on those least likely to gain access without federal help.

As support of both research and students increased during the 1960s, a third rationale for *institutional support* began to evolve. If it was important to conduct research or to educate, then it was important that the institutions be properly equipped to do the job. Through construction grants, funds for support activities such as libraries, or support for particular departments, the federal government began to concern itself with the financial needs of the institutions of higher education themselves.

The rapid increase in research funding, student aid, and institutional support, coupled as it was with a rise in state and private support for higher education, was a basic factor in the enormous growth of the 1950s and 1960s.

The Dynamics of Federal Funding

The growth in significance of federal support has been remarkable (see Figure 1). During this twenty-five year span,
total private, state, and federal expenditures for higher education grew three times as fast as the Gross National Product (GNP) of the United States.[9]

The first widespread involvement of the federal government in the postwar period was in academic science.
Whereas, prior to the war, university research had totaled
$15 million and had been mainly agricultural, by 1970 it
covered an enormous range of activities and totaled over
100 times that level.[10] Three major trends are evident in the
25 years of federal support of academic research: steady
growth; the gradual shift from military to civilian sponsorship; and the inclusion of additional fields of study, more
sponsoring agencies, and greater numbers of universities receiving research grants.[11]

The federal government became a main agent in the surge
of American research and scholarship to world leadership
in one field after another (see Figure 2). First the Defense
Department and the National Science Foundation (1950)
concerned themselves with science, as did the Atomic Energy
Commission and later the National Aeronautics and Space
Administration. Then medical research began to expand
rapidly in the 1950s, under the patronage of the venerable
Public Health Service and its offspring, the National Institutes of Health, which later expanded its support to include
the social sciences. In 1965, two additional fields, considerably removed from the hard sciences, began to receive federal
support with the establishment of the National Endowment
for the Arts and Humanities. In 1972, the National Institute for Education was established to upgrade the research

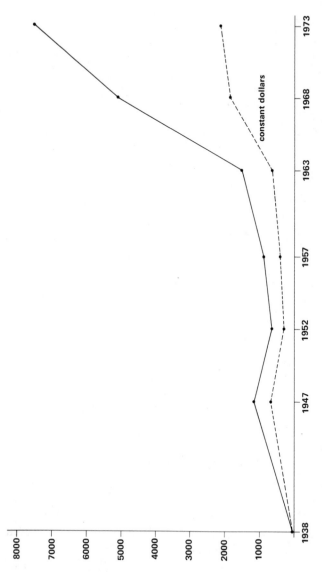

Figure 1. Total Federal Expenditures for Higher Education, Fiscal Years 1938–1973 (in millions of dollars).[12]

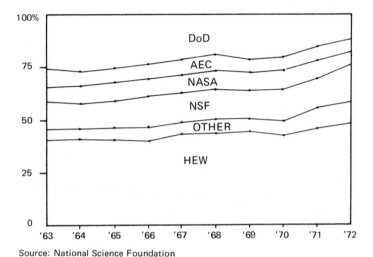

Source: National Science Foundation

Figure 2. Federal Funding for Research and Development at Colleges and Universities by Agency, Fiscal Years 1963–1972 (in cumulative percentages).[13]

in that field which had been supported for some time by the Office of Education.

Only a small number of institutions have ever been recipients of any significant amounts of federal research grants. Eighty-six percent of all research funds go to the top 100 universities. But those 100 have become models for almost all institutions, and faculty standards everywhere have been influenced by this reinforcement of the emphasis on research and publication.[14]

After a period of uncertainty, when federal funding in constant dollars declined, research support again appears headed upward (see Figure 3). Still not completely resolved are questions of the proper balance between basic and applied research and the role of the universities in each, par-

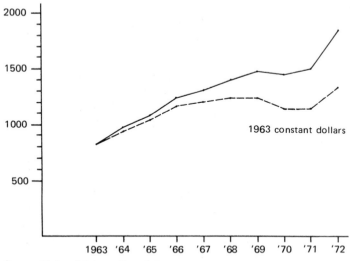

Source: National Science Foundation

Figure 3. Total Federal Funding for Research and Development at Colleges and Universities, Fiscal Years 1963–1972 (in millions of dollars).[13]

ticularly with regard to the new fields of national concern such as the environment or energy.

Some precedent for the federal interest in *student aid* existed in the New Deal's National Youth Administration which had provided college work-study funds.[15] The large-scale federal support of students really began in 1944 with the GI Bill, which was intended at first to help the readjustment of veterans (see Figure 4). Because it had no academic requirements for eligibility (other than admission to a certified program), it had a major influence on the public conception of who should be eligible for college entrance and student aid. At its peak in 1948, GI Bill expenditures for

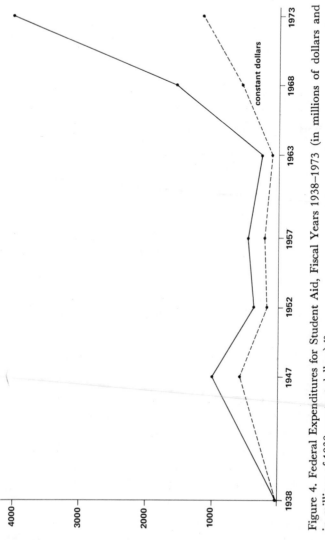

Figure 4. Federal Expenditures for Student Aid, Fiscal Years 1938–1973 (in millions of dollars and in millions of 1938 constant dollars).[12]

education reached $2.8 billion, and supported over a million college students, or one out of every two male students, as well as even larger numbers of students enrolled in vocational programs.[16] It is still the largest program, representing over 40 percent of federal student aid.

In the 1950s, the number of GI Bill beneficiaries dropped off. At the same time, graduate fellowships and traineeships, funded by a variety of federal agencies in response to their concerns over trained manpower, grew rapidly until 1968 when, under the shadow of oversupply, they began to diminish.[17]

During the 1960s, three new trends developed. A variety of new programs were established which, with the resurgence of the GI Bill, meant substantial funding growth. Increasingly, programs were focused on students from low-income families (Social Security Student Benefits, Work-Study, Educational Opportunity Grants, Talent Search, Upward Bound, and even to a degree the GI Bill because of changes in the makeup of the Armed Forces).[18] The newer programs, with the exception of Social Security, provided blocks of funding to the colleges and universities, which then provided aid to the students. A major reversal of this trend occurred with the establishment of the Basic Educational Opportunity Grant Program in 1972, which, like the GI Bill or Social Security, provides funding directly to the student (see Table 1).

There are a number of basic questions ahead: What is to be the federal interest in support of graduate education? Will emphasis shift to programs of direct funding of students as opposed to programs where the institution acts as an intermediary? What will be the future role of the GI Bill as the Department of Defense shifts to a smaller and volun-

Table 1. Federal Outlays for Undergraduate and Graduate Student Support by Agency and Program, Fiscal 1972 (in millions)[19]

Agencies and programs	Outlay
Health, Education and Welfare	
Office of Education	
Educational Opportunity Grants	$ 168
Work/Study Grants	250
Guaranteed Student Loans	227
Direct Student Loans	286
Social Security Administration	521
National Institutes of Health	207
Health Agencies and Other	116
Veterans Administration (GI Bill)	1,437
National Science Foundation	30
Defense	88
Justice	23
Other	23
Total	3,376

teer Armed Forces? How should federal programs treat costs to the student, including tuition; and, as a consequence, should federal programs help students with the added costs of attendance at private or out-of-state institutions?

Not all federal programs continue to grow indefinitely. Support of *construction* is one example of the retreat of a federal program in the face of changing conditions (see Figure 5). A New Deal precedent also existed for federal

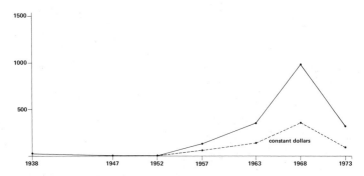

Figure 5. Federal Expenditures for Facilities and Equipment, Fiscal Years 1938–1973 (in millions of dollars and in millions of 1938 constant dollars).[12]

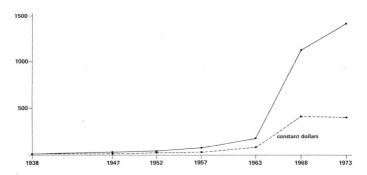

Figure 6. Federal Expenditures for Institutional Grants, Fiscal Years 1938–1973 (in millions of dollars and in millions of 1938 constant dollars).[12]

aid for campus construction in the extensive program of the Public Works Administration which lasted until 1939.[20] In 1950, with loans for faculty and student housing, the federal government began regular construction support. By 1966 almost $3 billion had been loaned for such purposes.[21] Grants for laboratories and research facilities were authorized in 1956. As the expansion of colleges and universities accelerated in the 1960s, direct matching grants were instituted first for undergraduate facilities, then for graduate construction, and finally for community colleges.[22] Obligations under the Higher Education Facilities Act reached an annual peak in 1967 of $720 million, but in succeeding years, as the perception spread that higher education had expanded enough, physical plant support was rapidly cut back, and there is little likelihood of its resuscitation in the foreseeable future.[23]

Only later in the postwar period did federal institutional aid become a major issue (see Figure 6). Not that it was a new subject. The first aid of this sort had been to found and then support on a yearly basis special-purpose colleges, such as West Point or Howard.[24] In 1890, when the Congress was concerned about the continuing health of the land-grant colleges it had helped to found, yearly aid was provided by the second Morrill Act, which persists to this day as a small, direct subsidy.[25]

A new phase began in the late 1950s and 1960s with a variety of institutional allowances, each intended to provide assistance to institutions which were meeting specific federal needs.[26] But during the 1960s and early 1970s, pressure mounted from the institutions to insure their financial health through general grants. The Higher Education Act Amendments of 1972, if funded, would carry out that evolution by providing a comprehensive program of grants to essentially all institutions of higher education.[27] The debate over whether to proceed with that program consequently marks an important choice as to the direction of federal policy.

Programs of direct funding have not been the only means of providing financial support. One of the most important—and effective—forms of financial encouragement has been the granting of tax incentives: a general exemption for non-profit postsecondary institutions from income or capital gains taxes, and deductions for individuals for philanthropic contributions to colleges and universities, the latter being of critical importance in the provision of almost $2 billion in donations to public and private colleges and universities.[28] In addition, tax exemptions apply to the parents of students enrolled in postsecondary institutions.[29] Over the last five years, however, as the interest in tax reform has moved to the forefront, various proposals have been advanced that threaten such large-scale educational philanthropy.[30]

The Proliferation of Federal Influences

Federal influence extends beyond financial support, either direct or indirect. As federal funding has grown, so has the federal tendency toward regulation. During the postwar years, the federal government has come to regulate, often unintentionally:

Faculty degrees, library size, and other similar academic concerns, indirectly through federal support of accreditation. (Originally a form of self-regulation, accreditation now depends on the persuasion of a seal of approval backed by the power of eligibility for federal funding. Accreditation is also used to control a host of other federal activities ranging from which institutions foreign students may attend as aliens to where members of the Armed Forces may go if applying for early release to attend college.)[31]

Affirmative Action requirements, both in admissions and employment.[32]

The accounting practices of institutions which administer research contracts.[33]

The financial plans of colleges and universities that apply for emergency assistance.[34]

Publication of the results of research sponsored by certain agencies.[35]

Student, faculty, and staff discipline with regard to campus disruptions.[36]

Beyond the examples noted above, a number of proposals for further regulation have been discussed seriously by the Congress. These include: the termination of research funds from the Department of Defense to any university proposing to drop its supposedly voluntary participation in ROTC;[37] the mandatory inclusion of student participants on all boards of trustees;[38] and the granting of institutional aid based on a formula utilizing a federally defined standardized credit hour.[39]

Recently there has been another series of federal decisions which have brought onto the campus an amalgam of federal powers and processes from which universities and colleges have long been shielded. Until the last few years, most federal law assumed that colleges and universities were different types of institutions that should be shielded from many federal programs. Lately they have been brought into conformity in a rush. Just in the last few years they have been:

Required to file income tax returns (even though not subject to tax).

Required to pay unemployment compensation.

Subjected to occupational safety and health regulations.

And, in what is probably one of the most significant decisions affecting the nature of postsecondary education in this decade, yet one adopted almost without debate, higher education is now subject to the regulations of the National Labor Relations Board.[40]

The actual import of a federal program often extends far beyond its original narrow intent. Just as was true with the GI Bill, Basic Educational Opportunity Grants are likely to affect the national perception of who should be a student. Federal research grants established a whole new system of rewards which not only reinforced "publish or perish" but also tended to encourage faculty loyalty to the discipline rather than the institution. The federal decision to use state agencies for the coordination of programs of student aid, facilities construction, and technical services caused a significant acceleration of state efforts toward creating agencies to coordinate and control *all* of postsecondary programs.[41] The recent intense debate over federal guidelines for state coordination of vocational and cooperative programs and state planning (the so-called 1202 Commissions) is an example of how even a modest federal intent can become amplified so as to have a major impact at the state level.

Frequently, federal policies in areas *outside* education have also had considerable influence on postsecondary education. The establishment of the Peace Corps and the changes in the draft are only two major examples. A decade from now, it may well become evident that the policy decisions being made now concerning Cable TV are to have important effects on postsecondary education.

In short, the postwar period has witnessed: first, a vast expansion of federal support and involvement, more than is generally recognized; second, a considerable extension of federal regulation and control; and third, a removal of the universities and colleges from their past ivory tower isolation through changes in a broad range of general federal programs.

The New Needs of the 1970s

The federal role in postsecondary education since World War II has served the country well. But the rationale for federal support during the 1950s and 1960s can no longer justify the same approaches through the 1970s.

There remains a need for a strong and vigorous federal role in research. But few shortages of trained manpower exist. The need now is for *better* training.

There remains a need for federal support in equalizing opportunity for postsecondary education. But federal financing for access alone is not enough. The new need is for access to forms of education which will be meaningful to the ever more diverse students seeking educational opportunities.

There remains a need for federal assistance to the institutions of postsecondary education. But this assistance should be directed not to the support of expansion per se, nor to federal assurance of a permanent level of institutional funding, but to specific reforms in the national interest.

The central concern of federal policy, therefore, must be the need for a more *effective* system of higher education. By this we mean a concern for the quality of student learning and for the relationship of that quality of learning to the resources used. The value of education in our society cannot be measured by simple quantifications such as the number of students entering college or number of dollars Americans are prepared to provide. Increasingly, the questions of importance are these: What types of institutions and programs are effective in meeting the educational needs of American society? How can federal support aid students and institutions in accomplishing their goals?

6
The Federal Role
in Postsecondary Education

There has never been, and we believe there should not be, an all-encompassing role for the federal government in this country comparable to that of a ministry of education in Europe, where national governments are charged with the responsibility for the funding, planning, and managing of postsecondary education. Rather, the federal government has concerned itself with *creating the conditions* under which the educational needs of American society are most likely to be met.

This is not to minimize the significance of the federal role. Federal funding has opened college opportunity to whole new segments of society; federal classifications for statistical purposes often define what is legitimate in education; federal regulations set limits on many academic decisions. If anything, the American approach is more demanding, requiring both imagination and prudence. What are the conditions necessary for more effective education? How can the federal government encourage and sustain these conditions without stifling initiative in the educational process and without undercutting the role that the individual states might appropriately play?

Forces for Change and Accountability
In the process of change and accountability in postsecondary education, each institution is responsive to a balance of forces. The balance among these forces is always shifting as both the organization of education and the demands of society change.[1]

The interests of students as they seek their own education are one force, the interests of faculty and of administration are others. The influence of outside educational agencies— accrediting associations and the disciplinary guilds—are also factors, as are alumni and donors. An increasingly potent set of influences extend from administrators in the central offices of multicampus systems, from statewide coordinating boards, and from the legislatures and governors' offices. In recent years, the several agencies of the federal government have generated a significant set of forces as well.

Action to affect the balance among these forces can take fundamentally different forms. Change can be induced by *incentive* approaches such as by the offer of funds for specific purposes. Or, institutional directions can be enforced through *regulatory* approaches such as Affirmative Action requirements or procedures requiring clearance of new academic programs. For a given end, either mode—incentive or regulatory—may be appropriate. But there is a growing tendency toward the automatic use of regulation without an adequate consideration of whether incentives would be preferable. A recent example has been the attempts of various states to regulate faculty teaching loads.[2] The trend toward regulation has been amplified by a general tendency to view agencies of government as having the prime if not the sole responsibility for the enforcement of accountability throughout society.[3]

There are, however, two very different strategies for achieving accountability. Strengthening the tendencies toward central control aimed at rationalizing and ordering the system represents one strategy. Strengthening the incentives for self-regulation, by making better information available, by increasing the choices available to students among institutions, and by encouraging institutions to respond to these choices, is quite another.

For reasons described in Chapter 4, the balance of these forces for most of postsecondary education is steadily shifting toward central control. In public institutions, effective control over decisions of budgeting, admissions, approval of new programs, promotion, and tenure is slipping from campus-based administrators and faculties to administrators arrayed above them in an evolving hierarchy of governance. And as state programs and powers are extended, both public and private institutions are affected.

In part, the determination of these agencies to exercise power more directly stems from their frustration with the intractability of the problems of higher education and the difficulty of generating a responsiveness to public needs on the part of colleges and universities.[4] But in large measure it represents a tendency inherent in any large organization for the forces affecting an institution to become permanently unbalanced, for those influences radiating downward from the upper levels of the hierarchy to become dominant, and for decision-making to become increasingly insulated from other influences. As higher education becomes organized as a service bureaucracy, only a determined effort will insure a continuing role of any significance in the decision-making process for faculty, students, campus administrators, and alumni.

Rationalization or Competition?

On all sides today there are proposals to create voluntary or enforced coordination among institutions.[5] The motivation is in part to enhance efficiency by division of labor, elimination of overlapping programs, use of common purchasing, assurance of programs and campuses of large enough size, and reduction of competition. All of this seems based on the assumption that there is one right way to produce a graduate, that education is like an assembly line with units of instruction that are interchangeable. If so, the only issues left for consideration are the quality of instruction and the cost per credit hour.

Even if one were to accept these simplistic notions, the assumption that efficiency will be achieved through this approach seems questionable. There is growing evidence that many of the benefits of close central control are elusive. Whereas it has been generally assumed that substantial economies of scale result from large campuses and centrally administered systems, recent studies indicate that the most economic size for a campus may be much smaller than anticipated, certainly under 10,000 students and perhaps under 5,000. Moreover, the central administrative offices for a number of the multicampus systems have grown so large that they themselves now represent a noticeable share of the higher education dollar.[6]

More importantly, those administrators and policy makers interested in improving cost effectiveness have generally failed to see that the greatest gains will come from concentration on effectiveness rather than on cost. Serious efforts to reduce the inputs to cost are important, but will result in far smaller gains in efficiency than attempts to match the student and the learning style better. Similarly, efforts to encourage students to be in college only when they are interested in learning what the college can teach will, we believe, achieve gains in both the effectiveness of learning and the efficiency of resource use many times larger than the gains which may be made from any of the factors presently under scrutiny.[7]

Too often, the problem of efficiency is thought of in terms of the need to reduce the number of Slavic language departments in a given city from two to one. There is an obvious waste of resources due to such overlapping of specialized and costly programs. Savings can be made through consolidation where the numbers are small and the students have comparable interests and abilities. But in the same city, there may be 10 or even 20 departments teaching English. A single approach to teaching English in a single setting would meet the needs of only a small minority of students. In such cases, the approach to teaching cannot be standardized because what students want to know and how they go about learning cannot and must not be standardized. Peer learning is a crucial element, as is a sense of community and a personal involvement, none of which is easily standardized or coordinated.

Surely there is a need for coordination in postsecondary education. Statewide planning is essential.[8] Articulation and transfer problems among institutions are real, and state agencies are the logical locus of such coordination. A number of these agencies, as noted earlier, have also demonstrated that they can be a force for diversity among institutions.[9] But this is only one kind of innovation—planned from the top to meet a widely perceived need. There is also a need to capitalize on the imagination of the many potential educational innovators who start from the bottom and see an opportunity to create a new program, a new style of teaching, or even a new institution to meet student needs. In the case of either kind of innovation—centrally conceived or grass root—as state systems grow older, as political tensions increase, as budgetary controls are refined, strong pressures develop that inhibit or erode new concepts.[10]

Coordination is necessary, but all too often policies intended to provide coordination work to inhibit mobility, innovation, and competition. When decision-making is re-

mote from the campuses, there is an easy slide from policy
direction to operational control, from concern for education
to concern for management, from interest in diversity to
standardization across units, and from incentives to regulatory approaches. We believe competition for students and
resources is a more desirable means of achieving public accountability.

Complete autonomy for the campus can of course be
wasteful or irrational, particularly if, as in the 1950s and
1960s, both resources and students are so plentiful that competitive forces are weak. Considerations of academic prestige
then played too large a role, so that every college opted to
become an elite research university and every student was
encouraged to become a Ph.D. New factors in today's world
of postsecondary education, such as the end of the draft
and the abundance of graduates in the job market, make
students more serious in their educational choices. Mean-
while, the tightness of budgets and the leveling of enrollments, both new factors, make institutions more responsive
to the real needs of students.

Even with these new factors pressing institutions toward
a sense of accountability, we do not propose sole dependence on autonomy and the workings of the educational
marketplace for insuring that the sum of the actions of the
institutions meets the needs of the public. There is too much
evidence that, given the chance, institutions and their faculties will be inner-directed—teaching what they want to
teach, lecturing in the style they find comfortable, and con-
centrating their attention on the students they find com-
patible. One need only note the continuing lack of attention to high attrition rates or to the measurement of the
effectiveness of current teaching methods. As in all of so-

ciety, educational institutions try to avoid the impact of competitive forces. State campuses, particularly, often look toward administrative help to assure an adequate flow of new students or the budgetary starvation of an effective public rival.

Our point is that accountability through competition can work, but that incentives must be strengthened. There must also be an effective means for insuring, through state and federal action, attention to those problems of public concern for which competitive forces work poorly. Equally important, we believe that accountability through central direction will not work and will bring in its wake new dangers to the freedoms so necessary in education. Therefore, in structuring both state and federal programs, the critical question is how to create incentives effective enough to achieve the broad, publicly determined goals while encouraging decentralized initiative and imagination to determine the specific institutional mission and methods. Rather than telling people what to do, federal efforts should create pressures and incentives that encourage educators to rethink for themselves what they are doing.

For competition to work, differences among institutions and programs must be apparent. There is a good deal of evidence to suggest that when information is available, students are sensitive to the differences among institutions and to the effectiveness of the education they offer. Undergraduates sensibly sort themselves as much by the environment for learning provided through an institution as by the courses offered. GI Bill students did not turn out to be as overly narrow in their educational choices as many had predicted. Graduate students have for some time tended to shift from areas of oversupply to areas where they perceive better career opportunities. Given choice, they shift from less effective programs. Once the opportunity was opened to black students, they moved toward a new mobility across a broad range of institutions.[11]

We believe the need for centralization and rationalization has been overestimated and its dangers underestimated. It is possible to encourage competition within the educational community to provide the maximum opportunity for the student and the vitality necessary in the institution for constant reevaluation and self-renewal. The ultimate test of accountability should be whether institutions can attract students and resources that match their missions. This means competition between public and private institutions, public and public, private and private, campus-based and non-campus-based programs, proprietary and nonprofit—but a healthy competition between educational programs based on their effectiveness, not between sectors or systems based on their political muscle.[12]

The Federal Role

Federal influence has grown steadily in the postwar period. Both the state and federal share of expenditures have grown until they each now represent about 30% of the total (see Table 1). Any thoughtful analysis of the federal role must, therefore, take into account the role of the states. Theirs antedates the federal role, tracing a lineage all the way back to the support of the first American college by the Massachusetts Bay Colony in 1636.

But, historically, the state and federal roles have been very different. Basically, state governments have been operators of certain of the institutions of higher education and the federal government has been a funding agency for

Table 1. Major Sources of Income for Colleges, Universities and Proprietary Educational Institutions, 1971–1972 (in billions)

Sources of Income	Institutional Support	Student Aid	Total Support	Percent of Total
Student payments for tuition and other fees	$10.6	$(4.2)	$ 6.2	20.8%
State and local government	8.8	.3	9.1	30.5
Federal government	4.6	3.7	8.3	27.9
Gifts and endowment earnings	2.5	.2	2.7	9.1
Auxiliary enterprises and other activities	3.5	–	3.5	11.7
Total	$29.8		$29.8	100.0%

Source: Unpublished data of the National Commission on the Financing of Post-Secondary Education.

special concerns. There has not, however, been a single federal-state division of labor. In university-based research, for instance, the federal government is dominant in funding, planning, and evaluation, while states play a supporting role only. In the field of civil rights, federal regulatory powers are used to force institutions and states to alter policies of racial discrimination. In the heyday of construction support, the federal government served as a supplementary funding agency, helping to support hard-pressed institutional or state capital budgets.

We believe there should be consciously different federal and state roles and that the relationship between them should vary depending on the specific objective being pursued. There are some aspects of postsecondary education where the federal government is the only agency of government charged with the responsibility for action (as in Affirmative Action or ROTC) and others (such as research) where it is the most logical agency. But there are also roles that we believe to be inappropriate—for example extending its role as a direct operator or as a general financial patron of institutions.

The federal government should not operate as a fifty-first state. As federal agencies become more deeply involved in postsecondary education, there is a natural temptation for them to slide into regulation of the organization and operation of institutions (in response to the frustrations felt within the federal government) or into general subsidies (in response to pressures from the colleges and universities). We believe this would be both ineffective and dangerous. For the public institutions this would mean that federal funds would to a large extent substitute for state funds and that the institutions would be left to cope with the regulations of one on top of the other. For private institutions it would mean a diminution of autonomy and an increasing tendency to turn toward the federal government rather than the education marketplace for direction. For the federal government it would mean the need to develop federal standards defining eligibility (with the need for a federally defined credit hour or standard of enrollment) as well as a diversion of its attention and resources from its appropriate roles.

Because American society is dynamic, the federal role in postsecondary education must continue to evolve. More problems are becoming national rather than local or regional as society becomes more complex and Americans more mobile. Federal involvement will likely continue to increase. In light of the changing nature of the problems, it is important that there be a federal role that is effective without imposing a new level of bureaucracy on the American educational community.

The foundation for a new federal role in postsecondary education exists in the more effective exercise of three responsibilities:

The responsibility to preserve an open society and the conditions necessary for a free competition of ideas.

The responsibility to overcome inequities facing specific individuals and groups.

The responsibility to support research, development, and other "strategic interventions" necessary for effective service which no other level of government can make.

Role Number 1:
Guaranteeing Openness and Competition
The federal government has historically and for most sectors of society established the ground rules designed to preserve options for individuals and competitive conditions for institutions. Thus, in regulating relations among private economic groups, the federal government plays the leading role in restraining monopolies which threaten to destroy the competitive conditions of the marketplace. On behalf of minorities and, more recently, women, the federal government has intervened to begin to lessen discrimination in all facets of our society.

Now, in education, new expectations and changing conditions have given rise to a new set of issues. Financial, legal, and academic barriers continue to restrict the movement of individuals from institution to institution. Many of these, including admissions policies, nontransferability of credits, and lack of articulation, are beyond the pale of legitimate federal regulatory action, though they may be subject to federal incentives. Others, such as tuition requirements for out-of-state students, are matters in which the courts are now struggling to define appropriate roles and responsibilities. But some restrictions, including many of the limitations on where and when students may use federal student assistance, are federally imposed and can and should be removed forthrightly. In most instances, the direction of movement is toward openness.

In the case of movement from education into productive roles in society, however, things seem to be becoming more restricted. The trend, shaped largely by the roles which self-governing professions and occupations play in establishing certification requirements in various fields, is toward arbitrary increases in the number of years of schooling required for entry into a career. Here, therefore, we believe there is a need for a more vigorous federal role with regard to the activities of accrediting and licensing groups.

As noted in Chapter 4, the conditions under which institutions can compete on the basis of the effectiveness of their educational offerings are also changing rapidly. Two primary trends emerge. First, private institutions are rapidly losing the capacity to compete with the lower-priced public institutions. Second, the new powers of higher education—the multicampus systems and the statewide coordinating and governing boards—are, without necessarily intending it, reducing the degree to which public institutions compete with one another and with private institutions.

The federal government, we believe, has an important role to play in all of this. It should help, not in supporting private institutions as institutions, but in preserving conditions under which they can compete effectively with public institutions, for the good of the entire educational community. Similarly, in view of the expanding domain of post-secondary education, the federal government should be concerned with establishing ground rules for fair competition so that the process of education is not needlessly confined to a single class of institution.

With regard to the development of multicampus systems, the federal government faces new and untried issues. In a number of states, the consolidation of public campus control and the competitive pressures on private institutions may soon create a new problem. Is there a danger that they will become higher education monopolies? Should nonprofit conglomerates which provide social services be treated differently from profit-making conglomerates providing goods and services in the market economy?

We believe that the federal government will have an increasingly important role to play as an agency of "antitrust" in education.[13] A philosophy of antitrust need not mean that the federal government confronts such issues on narrow legal grounds, or that its approach toward state agencies be a negative one based primarily on regulatory remedies. Rather, in its posture toward federal-state relations, we believe the federal government should assume a new role— that of creating incentives which will encourage state agencies toward openness, flexibility, and competition *within* their systems.

Too often in establishing procedures for interacting with the states, federal attention has been devoted primarily to organizational tidiness and bureaucratic convenience. The federal government has attempted to insure that there are: state agencies to administer federal programs which include representation from all segments of higher education; a state plan for postsecondary education; and, lately, "compre-

hensive" state planning.[14] Little attention has been focused
on the impact these decisions have on the educational community, on whether the state planning that has resulted
matches federal objectives, or whether it results in more
effective education for the student. Attempts to control
state action through mandated planning often result in a
planning process which is primarily a vehicle for capturing
a larger amount of federal grants rather than serving as a
true measure of educational needs. Programs tend to become uncoupled from the reality of the campus, resulting in
such problems as the recent overbuilding of dormitory space.

Yet there are opportunities for federal programs that both
aid state agencies and encourage institutional and individual autonomy. For example, it is possible to devise programs
which help separate the management role of the multicampus system from the coordinating and planning role of
the state coordinating agencies. The latter need real powers
to influence institutional behavior without becoming another layer of institutional management concerned primarily
with the organizational or financial problems of the institutions. Potential federal approaches include funding incentives that encourage the coordinating agency to focus its
attention on the student's and the state's needs for education, such as:

Matching federal funds for state scholarship and fellowship
programs.

Partial federal support for a state fund for project grants to
support innovative educational programs in public or private institutions (equal perhaps to 1% of the state's budget
for postsecondary education).

We also believe that federal programs that fund students
directly should take into account some part of the difference

in institutional charges so as to allow students a greater choice, thus encouraging a responsiveness to public need by the individual campus, whether public or private, with less need for central direction.

Role Number 2:
Efforts to Equalize Opportunities

The federal government has played a major role in equalizing opportunities. Federal student aid has assisted millions of students from low-income families. Federal regulatory efforts have been employed to bring an end to the discrimination against minorities and women. Programs such as Upward Bound, Talent Search, and Special Services for the Disadvantaged support efforts to recruit educationally disadvantaged students to college and then help them adjust to college environments.[15] Direct institutional assistance, such as the Developing Institutions Program, provides additional resources to institutions where student bodies include high proportions of minority students.[16]

Nevertheless, the principal thrust of these programs remains that of a strategy of access supplemented by a strategy for changing the attitudes and skills of the incoming students to increase their chances of survival in the institutions they attend. Even taking into account special programs such as veterans' early entry, black studies and other cultural awareness programs, or special tutorial and support services, it remains an inescapable fact that the basic forms and processes of postsecondary education have changed little to meet the needs of these new student populations. With a few notable exceptions the students have been expected to adjust to the college rather than the colleges changing in fundamental ways to accommodate to the needs of the student.[17]

While many students will continue to benefit from existing federal policies and programs, the limits of this approach must now be recognized, and more basic, structural innovations undertaken in behalf of the new categories of students. For capable but "nonacademic" students more concrete, task-oriented modes of learning must replace the passive, abstract style currently institutionalized in most colleges and universities. For students who are talented but not at ease with the dominant culture and the institutions which transmit that culture—as is the case, for example, with many native Americans or inner-city blacks—new institutions must be developed which will turn their own cultural traditions into an educational advantage.[18] For the many talented women students who are barred from effective opportunities by the time and place requirements of contemporary education, alternative structures and new means of finance must be devised. Thus, we believe there should be a new federal role in supporting a second generation of efforts to provide new educational opportunities to American citizens, just as once, 110 years ago, the federal government provided the incentives for the creation of the land-grant colleges to meet the needs of another new student population.

Role Number 3: Strategic Interventions for Educational Effectiveness

Some tasks are best accomplished nationally, through federal action, because no other level of government has the perspective, capacity, or leverage to perform them.

Information collection, policy analysis, and program evaluation are all tasks which call for increased and much improved federal action. As to information gathering, it is easy to forget that from 1867 to the late 1950s the principal role of the Office of Education was "to collect such statistics and facts as should show the condition and progress of education." Congress strongly reaffirmed that role in the 1972 legislation but at the same time the budget for statistical work was cut without a clear appraisal of the need for adequate information in policy making. We believe that the range of programs that are necessary, the depth of analysis required, and the scope of debate needed in order to examine the "condition and progress" of modern postsecondary education far surpass the historical and current role of the Office of Education.

In research and development, another traditional federal role, past federal efforts have been slender and not always focused on key problems. Information is needed on almost every pedagogical and management issue—how, why, and under what conditions students learn; what result learning has on their future or on society's progress; how resources are used and to what effect—a lengthy and urgent list. This deficiency has now been recognized and a new initiative has been undertaken with the establishment of the National Institute of Education.[19]

Experimentation and demonstration, as well as the funding of new ideas and practices, are also tasks which the federal government is often uniquely able to perform.[20] National perspectives are often needed in the evaluation of projects; national as against regional or local competition is often required for proposals of high quality; and national incentives are required for investments in many areas. Thus, breakthroughs in effectiveness—including new measures of assessing student performance—are tasks which will require, in our judgment, greater federal initiative.

Finally, while not often the direct and explicit purpose of federal programs, the power of the federal government to attract attention to an issue or to provide a sense of legitimacy for ideas or institutions cannot be overlooked. The public statements of federal officials, the debates of Congress, and the reports of federal commissions create issues for the entire country to consider. Federal operations, such as conferences, consultantships, and other forms of involvement, confer status and rewards, so that a federal concern for effectiveness in teaching will help to reinforce the growing campus efforts to create a reward system for teaching excellence. Even low-budget federal programs, such as the program for language and area studies, can legitimate, as no other social force can, the importance of certain issues with a multiplier effect throughout the nation. The federal government can be a catalyst and a source of leadership for reform and innovation, or it can be a powerful force for negativism and retrenchment.

Guides for Effective Federal Action
On all fronts, not just in postsecondary education, the federal government has found itself dealing with problems of ever greater subtlety as the role of government has become more extensive and society has become more complex. Determining the effectiveness of a given federal program is becoming harder and harder. For example, it is more difficult to understand how effective federal aid has been in supporting the evolution of the black college, or what changes have occurred in student life experiences through

the University Year for Action, than it was to measure the results of programs of a decade ago aimed at stepping up the construction of new buildings or doubling the annual number of Ph.D.'s graduating in physics. Yet despite this greater complexity, there is a growing demand on all levels of government for evidence that programs are, in fact, producing useful results, that they are not producing undesirable side effects, and that they are doing this at a cost which makes the investment worthwhile.[21] Failure to demonstrate such results quickly can lead to disenchantment and to demands for more regulation, which, in turn, often leads to larger bureaucracies—a seemingly inexorable and counterproductive cycle.

Both the agencies of the federal government and the beneficiaries of its programs have important stakes in developing more effective means of evaluating program results. It is simply no longer acceptable for those involved to say either, "Leave it to us, we know what we're doing," or "Education is so complex it can't be measured." The process of education *is* complex, but it is possible to generate useful measures. Far too often, the goals of a program are not defined realistically and, when they are, frequently *no* attempt is made to measure the results against them.

We do not mean that federal agencies should become mechanistic in their approach to accountability, routinely applying standardized evaluation procedures to each program. In responding to the pressures for measuring results, there should be a healthy skepticism in the application of quantitative analysis to the evaluation process. There is a recurring tendency among those concerned with program evaluation to emphasize those things that can be counted most easily. These measures in turn become normative both for the programs and ultimately for the educational process. Education lends itself poorly to this approach. There is no single "objective" measure of educational success comparable to the return on investment used by the businessman to measure disparate enterprises on a common scale. There is a great need for evaluation of the effectiveness of federal programs in education, but much to learn about how to accomplish it.

What the federal government has done best in postsecondary education is to establish programs of student aid and programs of competitively awarded grants such as those for university-based research. For effectiveness and equity in such efforts, the most functional and adaptive system of federal involvement requires a plurality of federal agencies and programs. Our national penchant for simplified organizational structure makes the preservation of such pluralism difficult. It seems so sensible to place all research in the National Science Foundation, all student aid in the Office of Education, and so on.

But there is a danger inherent in bureaucratic consolidation. If all research were centralized at the National Science Foundation, one view of priorities for research might well come to dominate, one set of contacts with researchers could become all-important. It might become harder for certain types of new ideas and new researchers to have a fair hearing. It is difficult for any one group to anticipate all of the new avenues to the solution of a problem. Federal roles (and national interests) often conflict with each other. All too frequently the attempt is made to solve all problems with one program. Instead, there is a need for many focused programs, each effective in its own way, the sum of which matches our national requirements. There are unquestionably too many federal programs in too many federal agencies affecting postsecondary education today. In the drive to reduce the overlap, however, the needed degree of pluralism must be preserved.

When other federal approaches are employed, such as discretionary grants or regulation, care must be taken to limit the expectations aroused in the Congress, the Administration, and the nation at large. Many times the results are far from those intended. When government regulates, for instance, the regulated often gain control of the regulatory process. Regulation is best used sparingly and reserved for those circumstances where no other means to insure goals of equity are available. The federal bureaucracy is a clumsy and blunt instrument for social action, not readily adapted to delicate adjustments in the education community.

Before action is taken, there is a need for the gathering of information, for analysis, and for debate. For the segment of society supposedly devoted to the practice of scholarship, the statistical data on higher education and the related research studies necessary for planning are embarrassingly thin. Some of the most significant federal programs in higher education have been instituted with little or none of the careful analysis necessary to determine what unexpected consequences might result.[22] Too often, the organized higher education community itself has stifled debate, preferring the appearance of unanimity to the benefits of an open consideration of alternatives. In many areas of postsecondary education, it helps to try out new programs on an experimental basis before support is provided on a widespread national basis. This is true not only for support of new types of institutions now seeking federal aid, such as open universities, but also for system-changing programs which can be tried out on a regional or local basis first. And, as federal programs shift from concern with expanding access to support of experimentation and innovation, there must be an expectation within government of occasional failure.

We believe the federal government is most effective when it uses incentive as opposed to regulatory methods, and specifically that it has been most effective through programs of student aid and programs of competitive research grants. Further, we believe both policy and operational considerations indicate that the federal government should stay away from general institutional aid or broad attempts at regulation in postsecondary education. If past experience is any guide, either approach is likely to generate a chain of events capable of inflicting major damage on the educational community.

Agenda for Reform

We believe there must be a new concern on the part of the federal government for the effectiveness of American postsecondary education. Throughout this report, we have tried to describe what that can mean in educational terms. In summary, we believe that greater effectiveness in postsecondary education requires moving toward the following:

More conscious and deliberate choices by young people as to whether to go to college, when to go, and what kind of institution or program to attend—aided by the widespread availability of information about the nature of programs and institutions.

Greater opportunity for individuals to return on a recurrent basis to a full range of educational programs.

More focused and more responsive institutions, each of which has a clear purpose and mission—all of which compete for students and resources on the basis of the effectiveness of their educational programs.

A deepening of the effort to translate into educational reality the social commitment that higher education in all its facets is to be available to and effective for all segments of the population—specifically minorities, women, students beyond the traditional college age, and students of limited income.

Increased recognition of and legitimacy for the role that proprietary, industrial, cultural, and community organizations can play in providing postsecondary education.

More resources for new educational enterprises and more flexible accrediting so that those with promise will have an opportunity to prove themselves—and more emphasis on the flow of public resources on a competitive basis so that ineffective institutions, public or private, may face the eventuality of demise.

More serious effort to improve the effectiveness of every type of program from liberal arts to vocational training through the clarification of institutional objectives, the development of realistic means to assess the achievement of objectives, and better ways to relate the resources used to the objectives attained.

A more open system of education and only such restrictions on the entry to careers based on educational credentials as are needed to ensure the protection of society.

We believe the federal government should play a conscious role in helping to achieve these educational objectives. The approach it takes in doing this is critical. Throughout the report, and often in greater detail in the various position papers of the Task Force, we have proposed specific federal policies, programs, and actions. While each proposal deserves its own careful analysis and detailed description, in summary we propose that the federal government should consider the following recommendations:

1. In allocating future increases of support to postsecondary education, the federal government should choose forms of assistance which maximize the incentives for institutions to compete for students, and minimize the risks of deliberate

or inadvertent federal intrusion into institutional operations. To the extent appropriate in each program, the question "Who gets what?" should be determined by student choice rather than legislative formulas or administrative decisions; therefore we recommend that, wherever feasible, federal support for postsecondary education *flow to students* rather than to institutions.

2. We believe that greater exposure of students to the productive activities of society outside schooling would help make college opportunities more valued and increase the ability of students to profit from the classroom experience. Accordingly, we recommend that the federal government place increasing *emphasis on work-study and internship* forms of student aid funding, and undertake new efforts to upgrade the jobs in these programs into significant productive experiences. Specifically, we recommend that 20% of work-study funds be allocated on an incentive basis to institutions willing to upgrade the work component into a significant learning experience.

We further recommend new federal legislation, a *"GI Bill for Community Service,"* designed to legitimate breaking the educational lockstep for a period of service in selected national, regional, or local community programs. The benefits, like those of the GI Bill, would accrue during the period of service and could be used later whenever the volunteer chose to enroll at a postsecondary educational institution. This program would supplement existing federal student assistance, and extend the concept of service, in addition to need and academic ability, as a legitimate basis for the award of federal student aid.

3. The issue in graduate education today is not growth, but reform; not the shortage of needed manpower in various fields, but the need for improved training in certain fields. The problems of the 1970s include the inadequate representation of minorities, the growth of new programs in institutions reaching for "university status" while institutions of acknowledged excellence decline in enrollments, and the lack of innovation and responsiveness to major social needs throughout graduate education. Federal concern, therefore, should shift from the quantity of manpower in various fields to the kind and quality of this manpower.

The interest of students in entering fields of greatest career opportunity, in attending programs of high quality, and in preparing themselves to meet real social needs is substantially congruent with the national interest in reform. Accordingly, we recommend that basic federal support for *graduate education* shift from fellowship and traineeship funds provided to institutions to *portable fellowships,* allocated *directly to students,* together with *companion grants* to those institutions which students choose to attend. We also propose that graduate fellowship recipients be selected on broader criteria than grades and tests, criteria which will be indicative of the contribution the student will make to society after graduation. We further propose the use of project grants to assist in the development of more effective graduate programs in social service fields and other new areas of concern.

4. For all students and all types of institutions, there is a need to know if the educational process is effective. In addition, the key to overcoming many of the obstacles to equity, social mobility, and cost effectiveness in postsecondary education lies in the standards and processes by which institutions assess individual progress and award credentials. Present testing and grading methods fail to identify talent beyond the purely academic, and predict mainly how well a student will perform at the next level of schooling—not his performance or contribution to society after graduation. Since the institutionalization of the credit hour as the basic unit of education, the processes of assessment and credentialing have been related more to time than performance. To meet new needs for equity and excellence, we recommend: (1) long-term support for the development of ways, going beyond paper-and-pencil examinations, *to evaluate mastery of proficiencies* needed for success in various fields of endeavor, and (2) support for start-up costs for the *establishment of examining agencies* capable of awarding credentials on the basis of the proficiencies individuals have achieved, regardless of how or where these proficiencies were acquired.

5. Increasing public and governmental pressure for performance and accountability in higher education has pro-

duced some new concern for efficiency in recent years, but has not arrested rising educational costs. Now, colleges and universities face the unpleasant specter of imposed management controls, such as uniform cost accounting procedures, which symbolize efficiency but bear little relationship to real increases in educational effectiveness. On the contrary, if such controls introduce rigidities into institutional resource allocation, they can easily impede progress toward increased educational effectiveness.

This situation has come about, in part, because of the reluctance of faculty and administrators to recognize its urgency, but also because there is little helpful research on cost effectiveness in higher education. Economists have tended to focus on cost factors, assuming that degrees awarded or incomes after degrees measure the results of education. Psychologists, sociologists, and others interested in personal development have recently begun to compare the effects of alternative structures and environments on student learning, but rarely in terms of the resources utilized. Therefore, we recommend that the federal agencies engaged in research and demonstration grant funding such as the National Institute of Education undertake *experimental, interdisciplinary research in cost effectiveness* as one of its major higher education initiatives.

6. Standards of training and competency in many occupations are essential for consumer protection. All too often, however, such standards become the means for limiting entry to careers. To remove unjust and artificial barriers to entering careers, and to the pursuit of recurrent patterns of education and work, we recommend that the federal government adopt a more vigilant *antitrust posture* relative to the activities of the organized professions. As first steps toward a new federal policy, we recommend: (1) a clarification of federal law and regulatory responsibility as between the Department of Justice, the Federal Trade Commission, and the mission-oriented domestic agencies relative to the activities of nonprofit professional groups; and (2) a thorough investigation, by responsible federal agencies, of (a) requirements for graduation from professionally accredited institutions used as prerequisites for admission to certify-

ing and licensing examinations, and (b) other examination requirements unrelated to the proficiencies needed to practice one's profession competently.

7. In many programs, the federal government has delegated its responsibility for determining the eligibility of institutions for federal funds to accrediting agencies, which render judgments on the basis of interests and standards which often differ from those appropriate to the national interest. In order to adopt a more neutral and equitable national posture regarding the range and type of institutions and programs capable of providing postsecondary education, and in order to clarify the roles and interests of all parties engaged in evaluating institutions—including the academic professions, regional collections of academic institutions, the states, and the federal government—we recommend that the *process of determining eligibility for federal funds be clearly* distinguished and *separated from the process by which accrediting agencies judge institutional performance.* To this end, we propose a national procedure for determining eligibility based primarily on an institutional disclosure statement that provides more useful information for the potential student and the general public and an administrative judgment that an institution has the capacity to perform its stated mission. There still remains the important traditional role of the accrediting agencies in assisting institutions to determine how well they are performing their missions. To help develop new skills in this area, we recommend federal support for research and development of performance criteria and new assessment techniques.

8. To develop the data and analysis needed for informed policy-making, we recommend creating *a new statistical agency* and *an upgraded analysis and data collection policy* for the Education Division of the Department of Health, Education, and Welfare. Collection of information was the first role assigned to the Office of Education, but today the resources, capabilities, and support for this task fall far short of comparable federal efforts to generate information for policy-making in economic policy, employment, or science. The new statistical agency, designed to establish a new leadership role of the federal government in the collec-

tion of educational data, should integrate the policy analysis and data collection functions, now performed by separate units. A revised data collection policy should include an expansion of the universe of educating agencies on which data is collected and a greatly increased emphasis on longitudinal studies of the effect of different educational environments on students.

9. In the last two decades, the federal government has spent billions of dollars on efforts to bring educational technology into useful service. Unfortunately, the vast majority of projects have failed to produce lasting applications, despite the generally accepted belief that communications technology should be capable of providing workable solutions to many of the problems that beset education. We believe the reasons for this failure can be traced to an inadequate understanding of the conditions necessary for the successful application of technology to education; and we propose a *set of standards* which we believe federal agencies would be wise to use in assessing future projects that envision *the use of technology for educational purposes.* The guidelines are: (1) educational programs must be planned for specific target audiences; (2) educational objectives that are relevant to the needs and interests of a target audience must be clearly understood and agreed upon; (3) a systematic multimedia approach must be used in which both knowledge and media specialists are employed in the production of materials; (4) persons who are capable of learning to use the instructional characteristics of various media must be available or be trained to staff the effort; (5) clear and careful provisions for significant personal interaction (both student-student and student-faculty) must be made; and (6) evaluation and feedback arrangements must be used to monitor audience reactions and to change the instructional materials to suit learner needs. Where these standards have been met in the past, projects have been substantially more likely to succeed.

10. Federal incentives and funding have played a major role in the opening of postsecondary education to minority students. Substantial problems remain, however, and there are indications that the public commitment is waning. We

believe that this country should recommit itself to educational opportunity for minorities. Specifically we believe the federal government should: (1) develop a program of national fellowships at the graduate level with criteria for selection that will aid, among others, many of the talented minority students now completing their undergraduate training; and (2) continue the support for black and other ethnic colleges, which play a critical role far beyond the numbers they educate. The government should, however, insure that this funding is focused as an incentive toward helping these institutions achieve a viable and competitive role in postsecondary education without the need for permanent federal support.

11. Three types of barriers continue to block women from full participation in higher education and the life of society: overt discrimination by admissions officers, employers, and others; institutional barriers, such as rigid residency requirements or inflexible personnel policies; and ingrained assumptions about the role of women in society. In recent years, the federal government has employed its regulatory powers toward ending overt discrimination. We believe it should continue to do so until such discrimination is eliminated. But continued progress will necessitate *greater reliance on financial assistance programs* (e.g., work-study, cooperative education, graduate fellowships, and internships) which can open access to new careers and professions, and *incentive grant programs* which can overcome those institutional rigidities which discourage participation.

Finally, the federal government has various means for influencing the role conceptions of men and women. Its significance as an exemplary employer is widely recognized. Less recognized, but also important, is its role as an investor in training, education, and service programs which help establish the values and attitudes society considers important. For example, if programs in professional education and the social services were to recognize the importance of affective values and attitudes, these services would improve. Since there is a widespread association of women with many of these values, the role of women would also be held in higher esteem. We recommend, therefore, that the federal government *review existing programs of support for training and professional education* to consider whether they really prepare individual professionals who are simultaneously skilled, effective, *and* oriented to the service of others.

12. There is widespread agreement that the encouragement of recurrent patterns of education should become a new national priority. Yet few agree on what strategies should be employed to finance access to postsecondary education on a life-long basis. Many employers have some provision for financing recurrent opportunities for their employees. The Social Security system, pension funds, unemployment compensation, federal student assistance programs, and new concepts such as the creation of an educational trust fund have all been put forward in recent years, each with a different set of training, educational, and "quality of life" purposes in mind, and each affecting different constituencies. Accordingly, we recommend that the Secretary of Health, Education, and Welfare commission a *comprehensive analysis* of these financing strategies, develop a forum for the public discussion of the competing priorities and diverse interests involved, and develop an effective program of *financing of students during recurrent periods of education*.

13. We recommend that the federal government initiate a new policy of *encouraging states to develop strategies for accountability* which rely more on *competitive forces and incentive approaches* rather than on direct and detailed management of institutions from the level of state systems or statewide agencies. We propose that where both state multicampus systems and statewide coordinating agencies exist, federal policy distinguish clearly between the two. Specifically, we propose three initiatives: (1) federal matching grants to states which undertake student aid programs which provide funds directly to the student, assisting the student to attend any postsecondary institution of his choice to which he can gain admission; (2) federal support on a matching basis for state competitive grant foundations, equal to perhaps 1% of the state's annual budget for postsecondary education, designed to provide incentives to institutions and faculties for program development and innovative approaches along lines determined to be in the state interest; (3) federal project grants to states for planning and

demonstrations of different governance structures and accountability procedures, including experiments in budgeting and institutional evaluation. Rather than simply funding the establishment of uniformly constituted 1202 Commissions, we recommend selective, demonstration-grant funding for different approaches to the state planning role.

14. The existence of public and private institutions, competing for students on the basis of the effectiveness of their educational programs, improves the whole of postsecondary education. To preserve the conditions necessary for this competition to continue, the federal government should give priority to strategies of postsecondary finance, particularly revision of its programs of student aid, which would *narrow the tuition differential between public and private institutions* without compromising the autonomy or independence of either. The vitality of both public and private campuses, their ability to differentiate themselves and the possibilities for creation of new educational enterprises are importantly affected by funds from private donors and foundations. In the reexamination of *federal tax policies* care should be taken to *enhance this flow of funds* and encourage a broader participation of the public in educational philanthropy.

15. Since World War II, federal support has created a vast reward system of resources, legitimacy, visibility, and prestige for institutions and faculties engaged in academic research. We recommend that the federal government now consciously address itself to the creation of comparable *incentives and rewards for those concerned with teaching and learning* and with the *establishment of new educational enterprises.* Existing agencies such as the National Science Foundation or the National Endowment for the Humanities should be sources for the expansion of the federal role in this area, as should the activities of two new agencies, the National Institute for Education and the Fund for the Improvement of Post-Secondary Education.

Throughout this report the Task Force has made plain its belief that it is to the country's advantage to encourage a more open system of postsecondary education that emphasizes diversity among institutions and competition for both students and resources. We are aware that there are many voices favoring more centralized administration, arguing that this is needed for coordination and the elimination of duplication. We have favored openness and competition because we believe it leads to both a more effective and more efficient system.

But we have favored it as well for even more fundamental reasons. High value should be placed on the freedom of the student to seek the path to an education of his own choosing. Likewise, high value should be placed on the right of an institution to succeed—or fail—on the merit of its own decisions. In light of the importance of postsecondary education to a free society, the danger of impairment to these freedoms, no matter how inadvertent or well-intentioned, is a cause for constant concern and thoughtful debate.

Notes*

1. The Implications of the Egalitarian Commitment

1. The analysis of "aristocratic," "meritocratic" and "egalitarian" eras of higher education has been used by K. Patricia Cross in *Beyond the Open Door,* Chapter 1, and by Harold L. Hodgkinson in "Goal-Setting and Evaluation." For a history of the aristocratic phase, see Laurence R. Veysey, *The Emergence of the American University.* Christopher Jencks and David Riesman offer a comprehensive treatment of the development of American higher education in *The Academic Revolution.* For an analysis of recent trends in the growth and role-redefinition of higher education in an international context, see Martin Trow, *Problems in the Transition from Elite to Mass Higher Education.*

2. Colleges were established by many religious groups, by wealthy donors like the Stanfords, and also by municipalities (e.g., the University of Cincinnati). Moreover, unlike the case of European higher education, there was the possibility of access for the exceptional student of high ability and motivation who was prepared to work his way through. (It is doubtful that Herbert Hoover, LaFollette, or Booker T. Washington would have been well-received at Oxford or Hamburg.) In general, however, even the very gifted, unless they were of privileged background, had little hope of higher education in America until well into this century.

3. The federal land grants to states for religious and educational purposes, dating from 1787, were especially significant for the development of state universities in the West and Middle West. For a brief history of these early forms of federal support to higher education, see Alice Rivlin, *The Federal Role in Higher Education,* pp. 9–23. The City University of New York was founded in 1847.

4. We arrived at this figure by calculations based on figures from various sources. Most estimates of this sort determine the ratio of students enrolled in a given year to a particular age cohort (e.g.,

---

* Full references to cited works are given in the Bibliography. Works of general interest to this study will be found in the section marked "General"; others will be found in the chapter lists.

18–21). However, since enrollment figures include graduate and older students, and exclude those who have entered but dropped out, such estimates do not reflect the particular issue of concern here, namely, what share of the age cohort enters college at a given time. To correct the enrollment figures for our purposes, we estimated the percentage of older students and dropouts. A second type of estimate was arrived at by multiplying the percentage of high school graduates by the percentage of high school graduates who go on to college. By a combination of these methods, recognizing their limitations, we estimate that in 1940 only 10% of the age group entered college; in 1950 about 18%; and in 1970 well over 50%. See "Projections of School and College Enrollment," Current Population Reports, Census B, P25, January 1972, No. 473, Table 2, and the *Digest of Educational Statistics, 1970*.

5. Jencks and Riesman note "extremely high drop-out rates" in later stages of the aristocratic period as a result of faculty efforts to "weed out the misfits" (*The Academic Revolution,* p. 280).

6. See Note 1, above, for a discussion of these periods of American higher education. See also David Riesman, "Education at Harvard," for a chronicle of the rise of meritocratic values at an elitist institution. Riesman correlates meritocratic screening of students with the arrival of James Conant as President in 1933. A similar trend had been apparent in the Harvard law school early in the century, and had already characterized faculty selection during the latter third of the nineteenth century. However, for most institutions, meritocratic selection of students began only after World War II with the influx of returning veterans under the GI Bill. A further discussion of this phenomenon is to be found in Jencks and Riesman, *The Academic Revolution,* pp. 279–286.

7. Dael Wolfle, *America's Resources of Specialized Talent,* p. 6.

8. Daniel P. Moynihan, "The Impact on Manpower, Development and the Employment of Youth," in *Universal Higher Education,* Earl J. McGrath, ed., p. 66.

9. Studies of the socioeconomic and racial backgrounds of students indicate that a considerable reinforcement of social sorting still

occurs by the selectivity of the institutions. See the data in Chapter 2 of this report and in Note 6 of Chapter 2.

In addition, there remain considerable inequities in participation rates by state. For example, as compared to a national average of 41 undergraduates for every 100 individuals in the 18–29 age group, Utah, Wyoming, California, Connecticut, Idaho, and New York all enroll over 50 students per 100, whereas Alaska, Maine, Nevada, South Carolina, Georgia, North Carolina, and Virginia all enroll less than 30 per 100. To some extent this is a function of per capita state expenditures, which vary by a factor of five between Wyoming, which has the largest, and New Jersey, which has the lowest. See *The Capitol and the Campus: State Responsibility for Post-Secondary Education,* Carnegie Commission on Higher Education, pp. 39–56. See also Carnegie Commission on Higher Education, *New Students and New Places.*

10. *The Capitol and the Campus,* p. 43.

11. There are 2,866,000 students today in 1,141 institutions ("A Kind of Higher Education," *New York Times Magazine,* May 27, 1973, pp. 12–13). The California community college system alone accounts for almost 800,000 students on 94 campuses (figures from Arthur Cohen, director of the ERIC Clearinghouse on Community Colleges, Los Angeles).

12. The *New York Times,* May 20, 1973, states that minority enrollment has increased from 434,000 in 1968 to 727,000 in 1972.

13. A small but significant number of new colleges for minorities have been established; examples are: DQU (Universidad Deganawidah Quetzalcoatl) in California, Navajo College and Navajo Tribal Community College in Arizona, Malcolm X in Chicago, Nairobi in East Palo Alto, California, Malcolm King in Harlem, and Third College at San Diego. Other colleges have taken on an ethnic emphasis because of their location in urban environments, such as La Guardia or the College for Human Services in New York or Federal City College in Washington. Others, like Old Westbury II, have redefined their mission to include an emphasis on minorities. Still others, like Alice Lloyd in Kentucky and the Arizona Jobs College, serve regionally defined disadvantaged groups.

14. Open access at the City University of New York did not mean access to any campus or any program for any student; rather, it meant that any student would have access to some campus within the system. However, the intensity of the debate reflected the inherent conflict between egalitarian and meritocratic admissions policies. Evidence about the success of the program is mixed. Martin Mayer in his article "Higher Education for All?" gives a sobering account of the programs at a number of schools in the CUNY system, noting that over 50% of the open admissions students had left of their own will by 1972 and that "a considerable majority of the survivors are doing badly." More optimistic results are reported by Timothy Healy, Edward Quinn, Alexander Astin and Jack Rossman in "The Case for Open Admissions." For further discussion see Ken Libow and Ed Stuart, "Open Admissions: An Open and Shut Case?"

15. Several such universities without a physical campus have been established, such as Minnesota Metropolitan in St. Paul, Empire State in New York, Governor's State College in Illinois, the University Without Walls, Union Graduate School (of the Union for Experimenting Colleges and Universities), and a longstanding program at the State University of Nebraska. Others, such as the St. Louis University Metropolitan College, are being planned.

16. An egalitarian thrust on the part of the federal government was apparent in the 1965 Higher Education Amendments' Educational Opportunity Grants, and also in the College Work-Study Program, originally part of the Economic Opportunity Act of 1964. However, federal support of qualified students on the basis of need alone had been preceded by the College Scholarship Service in 1955. The National Merit Scholars, a public but not a federal program, selects students on the basis of achievement, but gives financial aid according to need.

17. The Basic Educational Opportunity Grant Program, which was authorized in the 1972 Education Amendments, can be interpreted as a significant added commitment to students from low-income families. It should be noted that in order to qualify for this program, students must be admitted to an approved institution of postsecondary education. For a discussion of the implications of

this legislation, see Harry Hogan, "The BEOG Revolution." See also Robert Hartman, "The Nixon Budget."

18. It is estimated that in 1966–1967, over 70% of students entering two-year colleges planned at least a bachelor's degree (18% planned an associate degree, 9% no degree) (Alan Bayer, David Drew, Alexander Astin, Robert Boruch, and John Creager, *The First Year of College: A Follow-Up Normative Report,* p. 26). However, even the most favorable evidence (relying on the self-reporting of students) suggests that less than 40% achieve an A.A. within 4 years after college entry (Alexander Astin, *The College Dropout: A National Profile,* p. 10). Data on rates of transfer to four-year institutions are skimpy, but Warren Willingham concludes from the few studies available (from Florida, California, and Illinois) that between 15 and 30% of students entering community colleges in different states transfer to a senior institution (*The No. 2 Access Problem: Transfer to the Upper Division,* pp. 30–31).

19. Evolving definitions of "equality of opportunity" provide an interesting barometer of the rise of egalitarian thought. Variations on the most extreme formulation of this educational philosophy include: recent recommendations by the Panel on Financing Low Income and Minority Students in Higher Education that *complete* equity of results be achieved for all racial and income groups in rates and patterns of enrollment and attrition and in distribution of students among types of institutions (*Toward Equal Opportunity for Higher Education,* pp. 6–9); suggestions that random admissions be instituted in order to distribute fairly the benefits of attendance at selective institutions (see for example Laurence DeWitt, "A Lottery System for Higher Education," and the frequent public statements by Alexander Astin during his period as director of research of the American Council on Education); and proposals to bypass the schools as arbiters of status and income by directly equalizing incomes (Christopher Jencks et al., *Inequality: A Reassessment of the Effect of Family and Schooling in America*). For a firm philosophical base for an egalitarian philosophy, see John Rawls, *Theory of Justice.* For a critique of the "equality of results" school of education philosophy, and of

Rawls, see Charles Frankel, "The New Egalitarianism and the Old."

20. The extension of federally insured student loans to students in proprietary schools in 1969 has also contributed to their acceptance, as has their eligibility under the Basic Educational Opportunity Grants Program. A further argument for acknowledging the legitimacy of these institutions is their effectiveness, which often exceeds that of community colleges in training for specific jobs. For this view, see Wellford Wilms, "A New Look at Proprietary Schools."

21. Estimates of enrollment in proprietary schools vary considerably, and depend on definition. For example, an unpublished study by Ted Youn for the Commission on the Financing of Post-Secondary Education suggests that there are now about 1.6 million students in 10,540 "career, non-collegiate" institutions. According to A. H. Belitsky, there were 7,071 such schools enrolling 1,564,000 students in 1966 (*Private Vocational Schools and Their Students: Unlimited Opportunities*). However, much larger estimates are given by Harold F. Clark and Harold S. Sloan, who find over 5 million students in 35,000 "vocational and leisure-time" schools (*Classrooms on Mainstreet*), and by Stanley Moses, who estimates 9.6 million students in proprietary schools in 1970 (*The Learning Force: A More Comprehensive Framework for Educational Policy*).

22. For descriptions of some of these programs and other examples, see Samuel Gould and K. Patricia Cross, eds., *Explorations in Non-Traditional Study*, and Ann Heiss, *An Inventory of Academic Innovation and Reform*. See also the section on "Diversity" in Chapter 3, below.

23. As noted with respect to enrollments in proprietary institutions, estimates of the size and definition of the legitimate constituency of postsecondary education vary considerably. Stanley Moses, by including audiences of some educational TV, gives an estimate of 68 million students (Moses, *The Learning Force*). In such a field, however, it is difficult to draw the line between adult education and entertainment; should, for instance, regular viewers of the *Forsyte Saga* be counted as students?

For descriptions of some of the programs cited, see: "Rand Corp. Initiates Its Own PhD Program," *Los Angeles Times,* Feb. 5, 1973; "Firm [Arthur D. Little, Inc.] to Grant Academic Degrees," *San Francisco Chronicle,* April 26, 1973; "40 Million Newspaper Readers to Get Option to Study College Course in an Educational Experiment," *New York Times,* Sept. 9, 1973 (enthusiastic response to the first newspaper course has generated plans for a second next year; see *Higher Education Daily,* Oct. 1, 1973, p. 4). Other examples are described in Warren Willingham, *The Source Book for Higher Education,* pp. 384–385. It is striking to note in this context that "the Department of Defense is said to spend more on education beyond high school than all the state legislatures in the country combined, and General Electric spends more than any but the largest universities" (Jencks and Riesman, *The Academic Revolution,* p. 506).

24. See the forthcoming Task Force Paper on accreditation and institutional eligibility.

25. See the Task Force Paper, *Report on Higher Education: The Federal Role: Data and Decision-Making in Higher Education,* for recommendations concerning federal data collection.

26. For an overview of this dilemma, see John Gardner, *Excellence.* Some proponents of egalitarianism acknowledge the conflict between standards and equality of opportunity and argue that, if a choice must be made, the latter is more important. See, for example, Jerome Karabel, "Open Admissions: Toward Meritocracy or Democracy?"

27. The late Paul Goodman was long a critic of these symptoms of the bureaucratization of education (see *Compulsory Mis-Education* and *Growing Up Absurd*). Ivan D. Illich argues from a similar perspective that the only remedy is to decentralize schools (*Deschooling Society*). Criticism aiming to conserve but revitalize current institutions of higher education is offered by Nevitt Sanford in *Where Colleges Fail.*

28. This perspective is now shared by many administrators of higher education. For example, William Birenbaum, president of Staten Island Community College, has said:

The credit-hour time-grid must be broken. But this requires a different view of the organization of knowledge and the ways that humans may be exposed to it. At the college level there is nothing magic about two years or four years, except the magic of institutional habit. Prior individual life-experience counts for a lot. ("Something for Everybody is not Enough," Speech at St. Louis ACE meeting, October 1970).

For an argument against *any* form of degrees, see David Hapgood, "Degrees: The Case for Abolition."

29. See Kenneth Roose and Charles Andersen, *A Rating of Graduate Programs,* pp. 42–43, and David W. Breneman, *An Economic Theory of Ph.D. Production: The Case at Berkeley.* The "effectiveness of doctoral program" ratings do not seem to reflect perceptions of anything other than "quality of graduate faculty." In the 1964 survey, scores on both correlated so highly that serious consideration was given to eliminating the "effectiveness" question (Roose and Andersen, *Rating,* p. 19).

30. Laurence B. DeWitt, in his article "A Lottery System for Higher Education," points out that the terms "standards" and "quality" as they relate to higher education usually refer to the inputs to the process, that is, to the students themselves. He notes that there is currently no satisfactory way to evaluate what an institution adds to a student's learning or development during his attendance, or what types of institutions are most beneficial to what types of student. For further discussion of the question of "value added," see Alexander Astin, "The Measured Effects of Higher Education"; Astin, "Undergraduate Achievement and Institutional 'Excellence' "; Robert Berls, "An Exploration of the Determinants of Effectiveness in Higher Education"; Arthur Chickering, "The Best Colleges Have the Least Effect"; Chickering, *Education and Identity;* K. Patricia Cross, "The New Learners"; Kenneth Feldman and Theodore Newcomb, *The Impact of College on Students;* and Harold Hodgkinson, "How Can We Measure the 'Value Added' to Students by College?" The growing concern with the concept of "value added" is reflected in the recommendations of a recent report of the Carnegie Commission on Higher Education, *Continuities and Discontinuities: Higher Education and the Schools.*

31. The identification of teachers with their discipline and its perpetuation, rather than with their role as educators of students has been increasingly noted. See, for example, Jencks and Riesman, *The Academic Revolution,* pp. 20–28, 492–504, 531–539, and Nevitt Sanford, "New Values and Faculty Response," pp. 30–49.

32. For a history of this trend, see Michael Schudson, "Organizing the 'Meritocracy': A History of the College Entrance Examining Board," in which Table A first appeared.

Table A. Size of the College Board and Its Examination Program

	Member Colleges[a]	High School Seniors Examined[b]	
1901	15	973	
1905	27	2,077	
1910	29	3,731	
1915	31	4,941	
1920	33	15,266	
1925	35	19,775	
1930	40	11,470	
1935	39	9,083	
1940	44	17,377	
1945	50	25,680	
		by College Board	by A.C.T.
1950	114	63,352	—
1955	167	85,790	—
1960	428	400,000	132,963
1965	579	850,000	705,089
1970	850	1,000,000	992,724

a. Number of College Members of College Board
b. Number of High School Seniors Examined by the College Board for College Entrance

33. See David Riesman, "Education at Harvard," and Riesman and Jencks, *The Academic Revolution,* pp. 279–386, for a perspective on this trend.

34. Early resistance to standardized testing, exemplified by Walter Lippmann and John Dewey, is recorded in Schudson, "Organizing the 'Meritocracy',", pp. 51ff.

35. It has been firmly established that grades and tests (e.g., ACT, SAT) are highly correlated with one another, and with future academic performance—not a surprising result, since both reflect a person's disposition toward and prior success with classroom skills. See, for instance, W. B. Schrader, "The Predictive Validity of College Board Admission Tests"; James Richards, Jr. and Sandra Lutz, *Predicting Student Success in College from the ACT Assessment;* and James Richards, Jr., John Holland, and Sandra Lutz, *The Prediction of Student Accomplishment in College.* K. Patricia Cross also notes this in "The New Learners." Insofar as grades affect admission to and graduation from college, they play an important role in distributing privilege. However, the importance of grades in getting the first job seems to vary. One survey, which asked 270 companies in 1972 to rank five factors in the order of their importance in hiring (personality, grade point average, "self-financing" through college, extracurricular activities, and marital status) found that personality and grades were consistently the most important with personality scoring somewhat higher. For more technical jobs, grades were the preferred factor (Claude Shell and Floyd Patrick, "Grades Continue to be Stressed by Recruiters"). Another study, which surveyed 1971 graduates from the University of Colorado instead of employers, found no significant differences between the grade point averages of employed and unemployed graduates. Campus leadership was likewise uncorrelated to employment (Joy Rossen, James Schoemer, and Patricia Nash, "Grades and Extra-Curricula Activities"). Our own informal survey of personnel directors of large San Francisco Bay area firms found that employers seldom claim to place more than marginal emphasis on grades. See also Note 39, below.

36. Some institutions and a larger number of small programs within institutions do employ additional mechanisms for evalua-

tion, such as senior theses, oral examinations, independent research projects, etc. And both the elimination of failing grades and the use of pass/fail and credit/no-credit courses is increasing (see "Question Marks on Marks," *New York Times*, Nov. 26, 1972). However, experiments with techniques such as self-evaluation and peer review (as at Common College, Woodside, California), written "profile" evaluation (as has been tried at the University of California at Santa Cruz), and "contracting" to undertake a certain amount of learning (as at Evergreen State in Washington, New College in Sarasota, Ottawa in Kansas, Empire State in New York, Minnesota Metro in St. Paul, and Johnston College in Redlands, California) are still rare.

37. Data from Arthur Chickering (personal communication). For summaries of many studies of student-faculty interaction at various institutions, see Kenneth Feldman and Theodore Newcomb, *The Impact of College on Students*, Vol. II, Tables 8c and 8d, pp. 161–162.

38. One can argue that current standardized measures of evaluation shape what is to be taught, and select out those students who most readily accept the current structure of society and its tasks. There is evidence that more creative students are more likely to drop out (see Paul Heist, ed., *The Creative College Student: An Unmet Challenge*).

39. Donald P. Hoyt, *The Relationship Between College Grades and Adult Achievement: A Review of the Literature*, p. i. Ivar Berg has shown that for some jobs (factory worker, bank teller, air traffic controller), neither grades nor amount of education are predictive of vocational achievement (*Education and Jobs: The Great Training Robbery*). David McClelland ("Testing for Competence Rather than Intelligence") discusses a number of studies which show slight relationship at best between grades or aptitude tests and measures of occupational success. These include: R. Thorndike and E. Hagen, *10,000 Careers;* L. Hudson, "Degree Class and Attainment in Scientific Research"; and C. Taylor, W. R. Smith, and B. Ghiselin, "The Creative and Other Contributors of One Sample of Research Scientists." It has been found as well that nonacademic achievement in college is relatively inde-

pendent of grades (James Richards, Jr., John Holland, and Sandra Lutz, *The Prediction of Student Accomplishment*), and that non-intellectual criteria for success in college can be predicted (Anne Anastasi, Martin J. Meade, and Alexander Schneiders, *The Validation of a Biographical Inventory as a Predictor of College Success*).

For evidence that grades *do* correlate with later success, see Paul Burnham and Albert Crawford, *Forecasting College Achievement,* Yale University Press, New Haven, 1946. Also, evidence has been found for substantial correlation between grades and the prestige of the occupation held seven years after graduation (Joe Spaeth and Andrew Greeley, *Recent Alumni and Higher Education,* p. 167). (However, it is possible that when grades or tests do correlate with subsquent success, this may be an artefact because of their association with class status and behavior.)

40. In order to shift the emphasis from the *sorting* of students according to standardized norms to the *developing* of students according to measures appropriate to their abilities and goals, students must be in a position to ask questions of institutions that are comparable to those now asked of them by institutions. This may soon happen. A study group reporting to the College Entrance Examination Board has recommended that the CEEB "right the balance" by providing students with a "more accurate and detailed basis for choosing a college." This would be done by requiring institutions which use board scores to submit to tests which would solicit information on "class size, time spent in class by professors, the faculty-student ratio, the number of students who drop out each year and why, and a measure . . . of the school's social and intellectual climate" ("Panel Asks Wide Reform of College Board Exams," *New York Times,* Nov. 1, 1970). See *Report of the Commission on Tests.* I: *Righting the Balance;* II: *Briefs.*

41. The evolution of such measures as aptitude and achievement tests was of course indispensable to the breaking down of the aristocratic dominance of higher education, as noted above. And they will continue to play an important role in the identification of certain kinds of talent and in helping match students with the institutions most suited to their abilities and purposes.

42. There have been significant attempts to measure these dimensions of student development on the part of researchers such as Nevitt Sanford et al. (*The American College*), Arthur Chickering (*Education and Identity*), William Perry (*Forms of Intellectual and Ethical Development in College Years*), and the many whose efforts are reported by Feldman and Newcomb in *The Impact of College*. Although the results of these studies clearly show the interrelationship between "personal" and "intellectual" growth, educational institutions have been slow to respond by developing more appropriate techniques for assessing and facilitating student development.

43. See Chickering, *Education and Identity,* especially pp. 196–219, for a discussion of how different styles of "curriculum, teaching and evaluation" affect student learning.

44. The College Entrance Examination Board, in response to a growing constituency with new needs, is currently engaged in an extensive effort to develop new kinds of testing along the lines suggested.

45. For an overview of nontraditional alternatives to the evaluation and identification of learning, see Ernest W. Kimmel, "Problems of Recognition," in Samuel Gould and K. Patricia Cross, eds., *Explorations in Non-Traditional Study,* pp. 64–95.

46. In the Task Force paper on graduate education, we argue that "the main criteria for admission should include demonstrated motivation: a goal-oriented aspiration to graduate study evidenced by willingness to take initiative and set standards for oneself and by independent accomplishment in non-classroom as well as classroom activities" (*Report on Higher Education: The Federal Role: Graduate Education,* pp. 34–35). Examples of fellowship programs which already employ standards beyond the purely academic are the Rhodes Scholarships, and the Danforth and Kent Fellowships.

47. This is true despite evidence that, beyond a given level, grades (both undergraduate and in medical school) are essentially unrelated to measures of on-the-job performance. See Hoyt, *The Relationship Between College Grades and Adult Achievement,* pp. 25–30. See also Notes 35 and 39 of this chapter.

48. The federal government is already involved in these matters. Thus, it has lent its power and prestige to the traditional methods for evaluating colleges and universities through the accrediting process, without a serious consideration of its effects. Federal programs, such as NDEA or the programs of the National Science Foundation, have had an important influence on the standards of both colleges and high schools, helping among other things to accelerate the spread of narrowly based academic merit testing.

2. The End of Guaranteed Social Mobility

1. This popular view of social advancement has been prevalent at least since World War II. A 1949 *Fortune* survey of the general adult population responses to the statement "One must have a college education to get ahead" were 56% Yes and 36% No (Vol. 40, Sup. 1–16, September 1949). In response to the question, "If you had a boy or girl graduate from high school, would you want them to go to college or do something else?" 62% would want their boy to attend, 50% would want a daughter to attend. When the fathers were professionals these percentages changed to 82% and 74%, and when the father was a wage-earner, the corresponding percentages were 54% and 38%. At that time, the most important thing which parents thought college should do for their children was to train the boy for a particular occupation and to prepare the girl for marriage.

In a 1973 statewide survey of the adult population by the California Poll, the proportion of adults agreeing strongly that "college education is a must for a young person to get anywhere" was 39%, with 31% agreeing with reservations. (Reported in the *San Jose Mercury,* July 3, 1973.)

2. A survey by the California Poll (see Note 1, this chapter) found that 76% of blacks and 52% of Chicanos compared to 35% of whites agreed strongly that "college education is a must for a young person to get anywhere." There also appeared to be a strong reverence for higher education among low-income adults. Of those with incomes under $4,999, 61% strongly agreed with the proposition; for incomes between $5,000 and $9,999, 39%

agreed; $10,000 to $14,999—37%; $15,000 to $19,999—27%; $20,000 and above—36%.

A recent ACE study indicates that 85% of black college freshmen versus 73% of non-blacks most often cite as their reason for going to college the desire to get a better job. Fifty-one percent of the fathers of the black college freshmen had not graduated from high school, compared to 23% for non-blacks. Black freshmen also held higher degree aspirations than non-blacks; 49% of blacks and 33% of non-blacks planned to work for a master's or doctoral degree. (Alan E. Bayer, *The Black College Freshman: Characteristics and Recent Trends.*)

3. The University of California's alumni office has sponsored a billboard campaign designed to facilitate recruitment, the slogan for which is "Education: the Key to Your Future." The obvious implication of their statement is that if one goes to college, one can expect to have a fulfilling career.

Evidence that students take these expectations seriously comes from the American Council on Education survey of each year's freshman class, which shows that the desire to obtain a high-paying job is an increasingly important reason for entering college, until today it is a prime concern of over two-thirds of the entering students. (*The American Freshman: National Norms for Fall 1971,* p. 43.)

The same expectations are prevalent and determining as graduates seek advanced degrees. An Educational Testing Service study entitled *The Graduates: A Report on the Characteristics and Plans of College Seniors,* which surveyed 21,000 seniors in 94 colleges, found that of those planning to attend graduate school, 50% thought an advanced degree would enhance their chances for a good salary later on and about 21% indicated that their plans for graduate school were based on an inability to find a good job right after college. (*Higher Education Daily,* Sept. 10, 1973.)

4. *Veterans Administration News,* April 26, 1973.

Additional examples include a notation in the article "Lifetime and Annual Income of Years of School Completed," that a college degree is worth $200,000–$250,000. Table 41 of the U.S. Bureau of the Census, *Income in 1968,* shows that males who have finished college but have done no graduate work have incomes of 170% of the mean income, compared to 111% for high school graduates and 96% for those who drop out of high school.

5. For a thorough description and analysis of higher education's impact on an individual's development see Arthur Chickering, *Education and Identity,* and Kenneth A. Feldman and Theodore M. Newcomb, *The Impact of College on Students.* The Christopher Jencks–David Riesman article "On Class in America" is also useful for its discussion of the interaction between education and prestige. Jerome Karabel and Alexander Astin supplement this discussion with their examination of the roles of differentiated education in sorting people into positions of varying status and power (*Social Class, Academic Ability and College "Quality,"* pp. 3, 4).

6. At the outset it is essential to understand that the concept of social status or class is very complex, engaging elements of family, occupation, life style, and attitudes as well as income, power, and wealth. Christopher Jencks and David Riesman provide a discussion of the factors shaping our perceptions of class and education both as an index of and a contributor to social status in their article "On Class in America."

Social mobility and particularly the ability to rise within the class structure is strongly emphasized in American traditions and philosophy. An empirical analysis of the extent of such mobility today may be found in Jencks et al., *Inequality: A Reassessment of the Effect of Family and Schooling in America.* Jencks indicates that the correlation between a father's occupational status and his son's is less than .50; in other words, that a father can pass on about half of his occupational advantage or disadvantage. He also indicates that there is about as much variation in status between brothers as in the population at large (p. 179). Specifically examining the relationship between occupational status and educational attainment, Jencks finds a correlation of about .65; an extra year of school confers a status advantage of about 6 points, or the difference between a chemical and an electrical engineer or between a foreman and a plumber (p. 181).

Peter Blau and Otis Duncan, in *The American Occupational*

Table A. Percentage Distribution of Males by Intergenerational Mobility by Level of Educational Attainment

	Elementary	High School		College		
Mobility	8	1–3	4	1–3	4	5+
High Upward	15.9	18.3	27.7	31.1	45.7	53.1
Upward	25.7	26.1	25.8	23.1	23.4	22.9
Stable	37.2	31.3	24.5	19.1	13.8	12.3
Downward	17.1	17.2	13.6	15.1	11.7	9.2
High Downward	4.2	6.9	8.4	11.6	5.4	2.8
Total	100.1	99.9	100.0	100.0	100.0	100.0

Structure, also explore that relationship, and their findings are reported in Table A.

To some extent the interpretation of higher upward intergenerational mobility must be modified by an understanding that those with lower socioeconomic backgrounds are less likely to have educational advantages. Patricia Cross documents this trend in *Beyond the Open Door,* p. 7; her results are shown in Table B.

Dealing more specifically with the relationship between education and income, Walter Adams and A. J. Jaffe ("Economic Returns on the College Investment") found that young men with a term or two of college (40% of the entrants who do not graduate) earned an average 10% more than men with only a high school credential; men completing three or four terms (an additional 37% of the nongraduates) earned 19% more than high school graduates; men failing to complete the final two years of college (23%) earned 21% more. But men who completed college or proceeded further earned on the average about 50% more than high school graduates.

Richard Eckaus, who uses a standardized hourly income concept to make his calculations, arrives at a 12% annual return on an investment in a college education (*Estimating the Returns to Education*), which is consistent with most estimates—in the range of 12 to 15 percent. See Dael Wolfle, *The Uses of Talent,* pp. 74–101.

Table B. High School Graduates Attending Two- or Four-year
Colleges

| | Socioeconomic Quarter | | | | | |
| | 1 (low) | | | 2 | | |
Ability Quarter	1957[a]	1961[b]	1967[c]	1957	1961	1967
Male	Percent			Percent		
1 (low)	6	9	33	18	14	30
2	17	16	43	27	25	39
3	28	32	60	43	38	69
4 (high)	52	58	75	59	74	80
Female						
1 (low)	4	8	25	9	12	28
2	6	13	28	20	12	36
3	9	25	44	24	30	48
4 (high)	28	34	60	37	51	73
	Socioeconomic Quarter					
	3			4 (high)		
Ability Quarter	1957	1961	1967	1957	1961	1967
Male	Percent			Percent		
1 (low)	18	16	29	39	34	57
2	34	36	55	61	45	61
3	51	48	68	73	72	79
4 (high)	72	79	89	91	90	92
Female						
1 (low)	16	13	36	33	26	37
2	26	21	50	44	37	67
3	31	40	68	67	65	77
4 (high)	48	71	83	76	85	93

a. 1957 graduates, with 1964 follow-up; Sewell and Shah (1967)
b. 1961 graduates, with 1962 follow-up; Schoenfeldt (1968)
c. 1967 graduates, with 1968 follow-up; ETS Growth Study data
analysis by Thomas Hilton

Finally, it is important to note that while these studies draw correlations between education and social status, nothing can be said about causal relationships. There are no studies to indicate that the individual with a college diploma who may have a 50% income advantage over the median enjoys that status because of his education. He might have enjoyed similar advantages without the degree, based on his own creative abilities, aggressiveness, or other personal qualities which are rewarded in the job market.

7. These correlations were cited in Stephen B. Withey, "Some Effects on Life Style," Chapter 5 in *A Degree and What Else?*
It is questionable, clearly, to what extent the presence of these traits can actually be attributed to the higher education experience. It may be simply the case that people less likely to be on welfare and less likely to have mental health problems are more likely to attend college.

8. *Consumer Income,* Current Population Reports, U.S. Department of Commerce, Bureau of the Census, Series P-60, No. 75, December 1970. James C. Byrnes ("On the Growth and Financing of Post-Secondary Education: Who Pays, Student or Taxpayer?") found a similar 60% income overlap when he surveyed 35- to 44-year-old male college versus high school graduates. One should note, however, a possible bias in his conclusions, since the full income benefit of the college degree might not have been realized by the age of 44.

9. The *Report on Higher Education: The Federal Role: Graduate Education* deals substantively with the dimensions and causes of these initial imbalances and the federal government's influence in correcting or sustaining them (pp. 1–16).

10. The problem with respect to engineers has received particular attention because of the visibility of the defense and aerospace industries where dramatic cutbacks in government expenditures have displaced many workers. At the moment the market for engineers has improved. The *New York Times* of March 11, 1971, reports that with current drops in enrollments in engineering, conservative forecasters are predicting an average shortage of 10,000 engineers for the next few years.

The rising popularity of socially relevant occupations and particularly the zeal for social reform has turned many young graduates towards a career in law. Enrollments in law schools have risen from 26,508 in 1965 to 37,538 in 1971. Although the Department of Labor predicts that the demand for new lawyers will remain stable—about 14,000 new jobs per year through the 1970s—such predictions are complicated by the fact that lawyers have options outside strictly legal practice, such as real estate, finance, or stock brokerage. Factors such as substantial growth in the paralegal field, simplified divorce procedures, the spread of no-fault insurance, or Supreme Court rulings changing counsel requirements for defendants also complicate predictions. See *Occupational Manpower and Training Needs,* Bulletin 1701, U.S. Department of Labor, Bureau of Labor Statistics, Washington, D.C., 1971; and Carnegie Commission on Higher Education, *College Graduates and Jobs,* pp. 99–108.

The teaching profession has been experiencing reduced demand as increases in primary and secondary school enrollments have slowed. Wolfle (*Uses of Talent,* pp. 40–42) explains the numerical effects of the declining birth rates since 1957 on elementary and secondary school enrollments and gives projections until 1977. He indicates that while such enrollments increased by between 500,000 and 1.5 million per year during the late fifties and sixties, the numbers of elementary and secondary students will show no yearly increases throughout the seventies. His estimates are borne out by the *San Francisco Chronicle* of September 17, 1973, which states that according to the U.S. Office of Education, public school enrollment this year has declined by about 300,000 since last fall—from 45.75 million students to 45.4 million. Laurence B. DeWitt and A. Dale Tussing (*The Supply and Demand for Graduates of Higher Education: 1970–1980,* pp. 23–26) analyze the effect that such declines will have on the demand for teachers. They estimate an annual demand for about 145,000 teachers in the 1970–1980 period and project that if trends continue to be uninfluenced by the surplus, as many as 320,000 persons would be seeking those positions in 1980. The problem assumes special importance when one considers the numbers of graduates which teaching traditionally employs. Wolfle (*Uses of Talent,* p. 39) notes that in 1966 it took one-third of all graduates to fill teaching positions. The *Higher Education Daily* of July 23, 1973, indicates the stability of that figure, reporting that of the 735,000 persons receiving bachelor's degrees and advanced degrees between July 1971 and June 1972 who were counted in the labor force, 666,000 were employed by October of 1972, and 33.6% of these were in teaching jobs.

It is unlikely that the job situation for college graduates will improve substantially during the 1970s. The 1972 *Manpower Report of the President* estimates that 9.8 million college-educated persons will enter the labor force during the 1970s and that the demand for these workers will be about 9.6 million. However, of these 9.6 million jobs, 2.6 million will be attributable to educational upgrading, which means that college graduates will be filling positions formerly held by nongraduates. These 2.6 million will in effect be underemployed. Numerous other studies obtain similar estimates. See Carnegie Commission on Higher Education, *College Graduates and Jobs;* DeWitt and Tussing, *Supply and Demand;* and the study by Herbert Bienenstock, "Job Outlook for College Graduates in the 1970's" reported in the *New York Times,* September 25, 1972.

11. Howard R. Bowen and Garth L. Mangum, *Automation and Economic Progress,* p. 17.

12. Much of the controversy concerning whether the increased introduction of sophisticated technology will raise or lower the necessary education level of the work force is based on case studies of specific plants or industries. After conducting a series of such studies, the Manpower Research Unit of the British Ministry of Labour concluded that in regard to a particular skill group, some introductions of new technology "deskilled" operations; others increased skill requirements. The average effects were not great. See Sir Denis Barnes, "Technological Change and the Occupational Structure," p. 5. Similar conclusions were reached by Morris A. Horrowitz and Irwin L. Herrnstadt, "Changes in the Skill Requirements of Occupations in Selected Industries," *Report of the National Commission on Technology, Automation and Economic Progress,* Appendix, Vol. II, pp. 227–230.

13. Charles Silberman explains in *The Myths of Automation,* pp. 33–35, how the tremendous government demand for professional and technical personnel to work in defense and aerospace was responsible for about a quarter of the growth in industry's employment of those workers during the 1950s. Defense spending between 1953 and 1959 for missiles, electronic equipment, and research and development more than doubled—from $3.3 billion to $7.1 billion —and then reached a peak in 1964 of $16 billion. But in 1964 and 1965 this wave of expenditures came to a halt. While private industry performs three-fourths of all research and development, the federal government finances two-thirds. Reduced demand and unemployment of technical personnel has resulted.

14. Some job categories are precise both in who is trained as a member of the profession and in the number of openings. Such jobs represent a growing share of the work force—nurses, teachers, doctors, college faculty members, librarians, and the like. In another set of jobs, one can tell who has been trained for that role, but not how many are required in society—lawyers, architects, and so forth. In most jobs, it is not possible to tell either how many people are trained for the job or how many are required— stockbrokers, clerical employees, and most government workers. DeWitt and Tussing *(Supply and Demand,* pp. 11–19) provide a discussion of the difficulties caused by the interaction of supply and demand and the effects of time lags in processing market information to determine manpower requirements.

It is also interesting to note as pointed out by Silberman *(Myths of Automation,* p. 120) and Wolfle *(Uses of Talent,* p. 17) that both the Japanese and Western Europeans operate very sophisticated economies with much smaller proportions of college-trained manpower than we do, indicating again the ambiguity of the requirements for such training.

For further discussion see Wolfle, *Uses of Talent,* pp. 43, 112–117.

15. While it is our conviction that a college education is useful for police officers, it is also apparent that credentials are often used merely as a screening device. It is noted in *Work in America,* p. 135, that 85% of new educated workers accept jobs previously

filled by individuals with fewer credentials. Jencks (*Inequality*, p. 182) applies an interesting analysis to this argument. He demonstrates that "once people enter a particular occupation, those that have additional education do not make appreciably more money than others in the occupation. Within any given occupation, an extra year of school or college is associated with an average salary advantage of only 2 to 3%." Jencks finds that this advantage largely reflects differences in cognitive skills, and when men with similar test scores are compared, those with more schooling have no advantage. Workers with more education do not show superior performance. DeWitt and Tussing (*Supply and Demand*, pp. 16–17) describe how jobs change to require more skills when there is an oversupply of college graduates. Nelson, Pech, and Kalachech in *Technology, Economic Growth and Public Policy*, cite an Eckaus study, "Economic Criteria for Educational Training," which found that "changes in the occupational work force required only a 4% rise in average educational attainments, much less than the rise that was actually experienced" (p. 143).

16. There are several ways to calculate this increase; all involve some uncertainty due to overlap in degrees granted to particular individuals, labor force projections, and imprecise knowledge about the educational attainments of those who will be leaving the labor force. Perhaps the simplest way to obtain this estimate is to consider that with the present labor force of approximately 90 million, about 12.6 million workers (14%) presently are college graduates. By 1980 an additional 10 million college graduates will enter the labor force, which at that time will be about 100 million (U.S. Bureau of Labor Statistics, Special Labor Force Report No. 119, *Labor Force Projections to 1985*). Since those leaving the labor force during this period will be predominantly from the highest age brackets, which also have the lowest percentages of degree holders, it is reasonable to expect that the proportion of the work force holding college degrees will be somewhere in the upper twenties by 1980.

17. Although the data on college enrollments and degrees awarded in foreign countries tends to be scattered, one can draw some rough comparisons with the United States. In Sweden, for ex-

ample, where the percentage of 20-year-olds passing the gymna-sium-leaving examination in 1968 was 23% and where the per-centage of all 19- to 24-year-olds in higher education was 11% in 1964 (compared to similar college enrollment rates in the United States for that period of between 35% and 40%), there has been a marked concern for many years about an oversupply of graduates. And this is in an economy considered to be one of the most advanced, well into the postindustrial era of a knowledge-based economy. See Barbara Burn, *Higher Education in Nine Countries.*

18. Similar labor force changes are foreseen by Bowen and Man-gum *(Automation and Progress,* pp. 62–66) drawing on Bureau of Labor Statistics data for the years 1964 and 1975 (projected). Andrew F. Brimmer anticipates labor force restructuring for as late as 1980 in his article "The Economic Outlook and the Future of the Negro College." For additional estimates of changes by occupation until 1980, see *Time* Magazine, May 24, 1971, p. 52, and *Occupational Outlook Handbook, 1972–73,* Bureau of Labor Statistics, Washington, D.C.

19. A description of how this calculation was made can be found in Note 4 of Chapter 1.

20. Figures on the teaching profession are from the *New York Times,* Aug. 5, 1973.

DeWitt and Tussing *(Supply and Demand,* p. 8) suggest that the underemployment of college graduates, a very difficult phe-nomenon to measure, may be voluntary in the sense that students feel they have a better chance of getting a good job if they have a credential, even if the job has little or no relation to their field of study. They may thus use the credential to obtain a job for which they are, strictly speaking, overqualified. Bowen and Man-gum *(Automation and Progress,* pp. 17–18), Eva Mueller *(Techno-logical Advance in an Expanding Economy,* p. 11), and Silberman *(Myths of Automation,* pp. 119, 120) all hold the view that it is indeed those with less education who must bear the brunt of un-employment. They substantiate their viewpoint with data and argument.

It is also becoming apparent that college graduates frequently find themselves working in fields unrelated to their area of study in school. The *New York Times* of September 2, 1973, reported that a U.S. Department of Labor study showed that 18.5% of the members of the Class of 1972 did not hold jobs related to their major educational fields. An additional 13% were in work only "somewhat related" to their studies. This point is also made by A. E. Bayer, H. S. Astin, and J. K. Folger (*Human Resources and Higher Education,* pp. 232–235), and by Wolfle (*Uses of Talent,* pp. 130–135).

21. See Notes 21 and 23 in Chapter 1.

22. See *Myths and Reality,* Bureau of Labor Statistics, U.S. Department of Labor, Washington, D.C., 1971; and *Handbook of Labor Statistics 1972,* Bulletin 1735, Bureau of Labor Statistics, U.S. Department of Labor, Washington, D.C., 1972.

23. *Earned Degrees Conferred in 1970–71,* National Center for Educational Statistics, Department of Health, Education, and Welfare, Publication No. OE 73-11412, U.S. Government Printing Office, 1973, p. 8.

24. The declining birthrate as of 1957 (see Note 10, this chapter) will begin having this effect in 1975. Carl York of the Office of Science and Technology, in an unpublished note, predicts that 1979 will be the peak year for persons turning 18.

25. One result is that the increased number of college-educated persons is in itself a force in reshaping the nature of American employment:

Economics departments in big business have been spawned by the availability of Ph.D.'s in this field.

Many engineers are working to find solutions for pollution, mass transportation, and other contemporary problems.

One particular instance is the creation—by recent graduates—of a number of new restaurants in the San Francisco Bay Area, with more decentralized and personal working relationships among employees and between waiter and customer.

Hopefully, this type of change from within occupational structures will eventually affect all work roles, so that, for example, a nurse can be more of an autonomous and professional person. *Work in America* offers an extensive discussion of the redesign of jobs and the humanization of work (pp. 93–120, 188–201). DeWitt and Tussing, *Supply and Demand,* pp. 16–19, analyze the process by which many jobs are reshaped.

26. There are already indications that the job outlook for college graduates may be improving. A College Placement Council survey released in August 1973, indicates that demand for this year's college graduate increased 15–20% over last year. Especially bright were the prospects for those majoring in engineering (up 30%), science and mathematics (up 27%), and business (up 23%). The resulting increases in pay offers ranged from 2.3% for humanities and social sciences graduates to 4.8% for chemistry, physics, and mathematics graduates.

27. It may well be, of course, that "downward social mobility" used in this sense does not at all reflect the perspective of the individual. This is presumably true of the middle-class youth who opts for a low-consumption communal life-style, and it is equally true for offspring of upper-class families who become, for example, scholars. As such, downward mobility does not necessarily reflect an inability to achieve. *Work in America* explores changing attitudes towards work, focusing on the growing dissatisfaction and alienation of young white collar workers as well as those in blue collar occupations (pp. 10–23, 29–56).

28. At equal levels of ability, children from upper- and middle-income quartiles are more likely to enter and complete some form of postsecondary education than their lower-income counterparts (see Note 6, this chapter). The consequences of financial advantage in terms of home environment as well as tuition costs must surely play a role in this, but psychological factors do so as well. Apparently, the expectations imposed by parents—or the lack of them—make a significant difference. Jencks and Riesman discuss this phenomenon in *The Academic Revolution,* p. 133. Leland L. Medsker and James W. Trent, in *Beyond High School: A Psychosocial Study of 10,000 High School Graduates,* p. 100, also found that those students most likely to complete college had planned in advance to attend and had parents who wanted them to go. Eric

Ashby, *Any Person, Any Study,* pp. 26–28, indicates that financial considerations are the reason for dropping out for only about one-fifth of the students who do not complete college. This suggests that the large majority of dropouts are middle-class young people who are simply unmotivated to obtain a degree. A. J. Jaffe and Walter Adams, *1971–1972 Progress Report and Findings,* also substantiate the contention that family income has a relatively weak relationship to educational persistence (pp. 21–25). For further information on the role of motivation and other factors affecting persistence, see Note 2 in Chapter 3.

29. David Riesman has observed of Harvard students in this regard that "it is the very opening of meritocratic competition to so many more contestants that has helped to spoil the contest for some young people of upper-middle-class origins. To compete to retain their inherited advantage would seem somehow unfair and would require a change in personal style" ("Education at Harvard," p. 35).

30. This anecdote was related by the couple to a member of the Task Force.

31. The expansion of access means that entrance is assured. However, with the decline of the legacy concept in admissions and with the growing reliance on grades and test scores, alumni parents are now finding it difficult to insure even access for their children to the more elite universities and graduate programs. Medical school admissions are an obvious case in point.

32. The *San Francisco Examiner* of May 13, 1973, notes that members of Local 3 of the Operating Engineers Union who handle big equipment on construction jobs average $17,000 for a nine-month year. The Bureau of the Census, Current Population Reports, *Consumer Income,* Series P-60, No. 84, July 1972, listed the percentages of operatives including transport workers in various income brackets. With incomes under $1,000: .7% of such workers; with incomes between $5,000 and $9,999: 6.6%; $10,000–$12,000: 15.7%; $12,000–$15,000: 15.9%; $15,000–$24,999: 14%; $25,000–$49,000: 1.1%. These incomes compare with a median household income of $9,700 in 1972 (*Consumer Income: House-*

hold *Money Income in 1972 and Selected Social and Economic Characteristics of Households,* Bureau of the Census, Series P-60, No. 89, July 1973). One should also consider that the median incomes for individual wage-earners must necessarily be lower than the incomes for households.

33. This conclusion finds support in Murray Milner's book *The Illusion of Equality: The Effects of Education on Opportunity, Inequality, and Social Conflict,* and in *Toward Equal Opportunity for Higher Education,* pp. 1–5. To the degree that optimal conditions obtain—where a license or degree in pharmacology, say, is available to anyone with the ability and motivation to earn it, an emphasis on such strictly objective criteria as test scores or credentials may enhance mobility for currently disadvantaged groups from low-status homes. Jencks (*Inequality,* p. 193) makes the point that if jobs were rationed on the basis of purely subjective criteria (e.g., interviews or supervisor ratings), those same groups might find their mobility even more restricted than it is at present. Of course an employer's arbitrary insistence on a degree may also unfairly deny access to better jobs to those who find themselves unsuited to academia or unable to attend college or complete their education.

34. "The Supreme Court, Mr. Chief Justice Burger, held that an employer was prohibited by provisions of Act pertaining to employment opportunities from requiring a high school education or passing of a standardized general intelligence test as a condition of employment in or transfer to jobs where neither standard was shown to be significantly related to successful job performance. Both requirements operated to disqualify Negroes at a substantially higher rate than white applicants and jobs in question formerly had been filled only by white employees as part of a long-standing practice of giving preference to whites." *Griggs vs. Duke Power Company,* 91 S. Ct. 849 (1971).

35. *Report on Higher Education,* U.S. Government Printing Office, Washington, D.C., 1971, p. 46.

36. The figures in Table C were compiled from the Bureau of the Census, Current Population Reports, *Population Characteristics,*

"Social and Economic Characteristics of Students." The enrollment statistics measure the numbers of blacks in "college" who are defined as full- or part-time students at universities, colleges, or professional schools. Attendees of proprietary schools are ostensibly excluded from the count, but here the definitions of institutions become very vague; this undoubtedly contributes to the discrepancies between the results of this and similar surveys. For a discussion of the many problems associated with gathering statistics on minorities, see Reynolds Farley, "The Quality of Demographic Data for Non-Whites." The Bureau of Labor Statistics ("The High School Class of 1972: More at Work, Fewer in College," *Monthly Labor Review*, June 1973) reported that the proportions of black and white high school graduates entering college in 1972 were nearly the same (47.6 and 49.4 percent, respectively). While this shows a substantial decrease in racial imbalance compared to 1968 (when enrollment rates were 56.6% for whites and 46.2% for blacks), these conclusions must be modified, as the Bureau indicates, by two factors: (1) the figures for blacks also include Orientals, American Indians, and other races, and (2) a larger proportion of young blacks drop out of high school before graduation—about 19% as of October 1972, compared to 13% for whites. 37. See Table C.

Table C. Enrollment in Higher Education (in thousands)

	Total Enrollment	Total Black Enrollment	Blacks as Percentage of Total Enrollment
1964	4,643	234	5.0%
1965	5,675	274	4.8
1966	5,999	282	4.7
1967	6,401	370	5.8
1968	6,801	435	6.4
1969	7,435	492	6.6
1970	7,413	522	7.0
1971	8,087	680	8.4
1972	8,313	727	8.7

38. Patricia Cross documents the figures for Spanish-speaking graduates and undergraduates in her article "The New Learners," p. 33. One gets an indication of trends in Puerto Rican enrollment by examining statistics from the *Report of the Fall 1971 Undergraduate Ethnic Census of the City University of New York*, p. 9. It shows that Puerto Rican enrollment in community colleges increased from 5.5% of the student population in 1967 to 8.6% in 1971. The enrollment increase for senior colleges was from 1.9% in 1967 to 4.5% in 1971. It should also be noted that 75% of the Puerto Rican population of the United States resides in New York or New Jersey, suggesting a general significance for these figures. In the case of native Americans, the *Higher Education Daily* of July 26, 1973, extrapolating from Bureau of the Census data, reports that the number of American Indians attending college doubled between 1960 and 1970. The actual 1973 census report (*American Indians*) showed total college enrollment of American Indians in 1970 at 14,191. "College" here includes junior or community colleges, four-year colleges, and graduate or professional schools.

39. Patricia Cross, "The New Learners," p. 34. Further evidence of rising graduate enrollments comes from a University of California survey of the nine campuses, which showed that, in 1972, 21% of graduate students were minority students, as compared to 6% in 1967. This 21% is specifically broken down into 5.7% for blacks, .5% for American Indians, 7.9% for Orientals, 5% for those with Spanish surnames, and 1.9% other. (Reported in the *San Francisco Chronicle*, July 11, 1973.)

40. The nature and extent of black progress over the past decade has been the subject of much controversy. Of particular interest was the Wattenburg-Scammon article "Black Progress and Liberal Rhetoric," which supported with extensive statistical analyses the proposition that a majority of blacks have moved into the middle class. Principal criticisms of their work (*Commentary*, August 1973, pp. 4–22) disputed the validity of their interpretations of the data and argued that even if it could be shown that in percentage terms blacks had progressed in relation to whites,

their absolute relationship had not improved, and black status remains deplorable. The Census Report, *Characteristics of the Low-Income Population: 1972* (P-60, No. 88), may give weight to the latter argument. It found that while the number of low-income white Americans declined by about 9% between 1971 and 1972 (from 17.8 million to 16.2 million), there was a small increase in the number of blacks in poverty, from 7.4 to 7.7 million. In 1972, about 9% of all white persons were in the low-income category; the figure for blacks was 33%. However, the situation does appear more optimistic for young, college-educated blacks. The 1971 Census Bureau report, *Social and Economic Status of Negroes in the United States,* indicated that young black women aged 25 to 34 with at least one year of college earn 97% of what similarly trained white women of that age earn. Young black men of that age and training earn an income 84% that of their white counterparts. This compares with incomes of older black men and women (35–54), which are 71% and 98% those of their similarly educated male and female white counterparts.

41. While the Wattenburg-Scammon analysis of black progress (see the previous note), extolling the remarkable advance of blacks over the last decade, may be encouraging, it should not be allowed to obscure the many problems confronting blacks who are not finding success either in education or careers. Furthermore, it should be emphasized that even those minority individuals who are successful face many difficulties which make their advancement particularly arduous. Martin Kilson has described the feelings of alienation and frustration of black students in the white environment of Harvard and the dilemmas and conflicts associated with black separatism on such campuses ("The Black Experience at Harvard"). Charles V. Willie and Arline S. McCord offer a more comprehensive survey of these difficulties, investigating social and housing problems, relationships with faculty, and problems in recruitment and financial aid in their study *Black Students at White Colleges.*

42. See, for example, Elliot Liebow, *Tally's Corner,* and William McCord, John Howard, Bernard Friedberg, and Edwin Harwood, *Life Styles in the Black Ghetto.*

43. An excellent example is a case *(DeFunis vs. Odegaard)* brought against the University of Washington in which a white law school candidate charged that his 14th Amendment rights to equal protection of the laws had been violated when the law school denied his admission while accepting certain minority applicants with lower test scores and grade point averages who would not have been admitted except for their minority status. The Washington State Supreme Court rejected his arguments, overturning the decision of a lower court. It is expected that the case will be appealed to the U.S. Supreme Court. (Reported in the *Chronicle of Higher Education,* March 26, 1973.)

44. Alan Bayer et al. *(Human Resources,* p. 16) indicate that black college students are twice as likely (40%) as non-blacks (18%) to depend on scholarships and grants as a major source of financial resources. Consequently, they also express considerably more anxiety about their ability to finance their education. The recently adopted federal program of Basic Educational Opportunity Grants based strictly on need should make funds available to all low-income minorities. A more germane problem is making the availability of such funds known to those students. Adequate counseling and information services are essential.

45. The role of family income is problematic for another group as well: the "emancipated" student, who is financially on his or her own, but is refused aid because of the family's financial status.

46. The Carnegie Commission on Higher Education report *From Isolation to Mainstream: Problems of the Colleges Founded for Negroes* offers evidence of the current and historic contributions of the black colleges to the education of black Americans and discusses problems related to their continued effectiveness. The Summer 1971 issue of *Daedalus,* "The Future of Black Colleges," Vol. 100, No. 3, is devoted to the problem and opportunities for traditionally black institutions. Additional information may be found in Thomas Sowell's *Black Education: Myths and Tragedies.*

47. *Report on Higher Education: The Federal Role: Graduate Education,* pp. 28–36.

48. The consensus of college and university officials attending a College Entrance Examination Board conference on minority admissions was that the commitment to expand non-white enrollments had lost much of its force. Because there have been dramatic percentage increases in minority enrollments, it was felt that many institutions might be satisfied to level off their recruitment efforts without realizing the 10% to 15% range which is the percentage of minorities in the college-age bracket of the population. It was believed that the greatest threats to increased enrollments were the proposed cutbacks in student financial aid and a growing resentment of programs which treat minority applications preferentially, admitting those students with lower test scores and grade point averages. (Reported in the *New York Times,* May 14, 1973.)

The *Wall Street Journal* of October 12, 1973, similarly reported feelings among educators that colleges and universities are no longer making a concentrated effort to recruit minority students. The reasons cited include uncertainty about federal financial aid, belief that the pool of "qualified" minority students is drying up (although black students of equal abilities are less likely to enroll than whites; see Table 3), and disappointment that the recruitment effort is not having a major effect on social problems.

The *Christian Science Monitor* of September 20, 1973, considered evidence of this waning commitment in its article "Cultural Centers Questioned." It reported that special black studies programs have become prime targets for universities caught in the financial squeeze. The article specifically pointed to the University of Wisconsin, which cut $90,000 from its budget support of the Afro-American Cultural Center on the Madison campus, the failure of Columbia University to replace faculty members who have left the African Studies Institute, and the announcement at New York University a year ago of its position against separate facilities, such as dormitories and social groups, for minorities. It must be understood, however, that these issues tend to be complex and many-faceted. For instance, the University of Wisconsin responded in that same *Christian Science Monitor* article that its principal mission is academic and that given limited resources, programs which directly support that mission must be given priority. University officials also cited philosophical bases for the cutback in funds. These were related to a resolution enacted by the university's Board of Regents supporting only multicultural and integrated programs on any campus. (Reported in the *New York Times,* August 9, 1973.)

49. The Higher Education Amendments of 1972, with their emphasis on aid to disadvantaged students, particularly through the newly established Basic Educational Opportunity Grants, are a strong beginning of our reaffirmation of the national commitment to social equity.

50. DeWitt and Tussing (*Supply and Demand,* pp. 25–26) indicate that it was not until late July 1971 that the National Educational Association, the principal analyst of teacher supply and demand in the United States, became aware of or alarmed by the impending teacher surplus.

51. Wolfle (*Uses of Talent,* pp. 47–49) discusses these contraining traditions which result in severe underutilization of trained manpower. In India at the time of the last census, 16% of all recent science and engineering graduates were unemployed. In the Philippines one-third of the medical school graduates never practice. It should also be noted, however, that part of this waste of trained manpower may be attributable to the economies' inabilities to create a market demand for the skills of their graduates.

52. The *Annual Report of the Office of Immigration and Naturalization* indicates that for the year ending June 30, 1972, 11,427 foreign physicians entered the United States, 480 more than in the previous year. Of those, 7,144 entered as permanent residents (1,388 more than in 1971) and the remainder came in as exchange visitors, students, or temporary workers. The Council on Medical Education of the American Medical Association indicates that in 1972, 6,661 foreign physicians were licensed in the United States, representing 46% of all newly licensed physicians of that year (*Medical Licensure Statistics,* 1972, p. 19). The numbers of Americans studying abroad is difficult to calculate due to the reporting practices of foreign medical schools. Estimates from the American Medical Association suggest that between 600 and 700 go abroad

each year, with about 4,000 studying at foreign schools at any one time.

53. Although the funding of such programs has been sustained despite administration attempts to pare federal expenditures, the impoundment of substantial funds is undermining incentives to correct health manpower imbalances. Documents submitted to the House Interstate and Foreign Commerce Committee, June 20, 1973, by the Department of Health, Education, and Welfare and released by the committee on July 25 listed $297,562,000 unspent on health manpower programs in the fiscal year 1973. Also of interest in this regard is the fact that Secretary of Health, Education, and Welfare Weinberger is proposing to change the format of such incentives from training grants to fellowships to be awarded directly to students in the health fields.

3. New Requirements for Effective Education

1. Eric Ashby observes that the "frivolous student" was tolerated two generations ago because he paid his own way and because there was no pressure for places (*Any Person, Any Study,* p. 29).

2. The Carnegie Commission on Higher Education estimates from a 1969 survey that "about 30% of all enrolled undergraduates appear to be less than fully committed" (*Reform on Campus,* p. 51). Of these students, 5% were "very reluctant," 7% were "marginally reluctant," and 18% were "marginally committed." A study by A. J. Jaffe and Walter Adams (*American Higher Education in Transition*) found that about 15% of students were in college "against their own will" (cited in *Reform on Campus,* p. 51, and Ashby, *Any Person, Any Study,* p. 29). Although the draft no longer represents an incentive for reluctant participation in education beyond high school, other forces do: parental expectations, and the expectation that college-going is a "must" to get a satisfactory job. However, the percentage of "involuntary" students may be decreasing as alternatives to lockstep college attendance are legitimized.

3. K. Patricia Cross defines "new learners" as "four distinctive but overlapping groups: (1) low academic achievers who are gaining

entrance through open admissions; (2) adults and part-time learners who are gaining access through non-traditional alternatives;
(3) ethnic minorities; and (4) women who are gaining admission
through public conscience and Affirmative Action" ("The New
Learners," p. 32).

4. K. Patricia Cross found that the new students are more concerned with education as a preparation for good jobs and incomes
than are traditional students (*New Students and New Needs in
Higher Education,* pp. 111–128). Since credentials are widely perceived as necessary for good jobs and salaries (see Notes 1, 2 in
Chapter 2), they are naturally attractive to the new learners.

5. Alabama A&M, with a student body composed mainly of blacks
from rural areas, reports that attrition has dropped from 65% to
35% after a basic restructuring of their program. The College for
Human Services boasts completion rates of over 80% for students
most of whom traditionally would not have participated in postsecondary education (information obtained from officers of these
institutions).

6. The only study to date of Vietnam-era veterans found that the
returning veterans were more likely to give as reasons for college
attendance "gaining a general education, becoming more cultured,
improving their reading skills, and learning more about things
that interest them. They were less likely to say that they had come
to college because they wanted to meet new and interesting people
or because their parents wanted them to" (David Drew and John
Creager, *The Vietnam-Era Veteran Enters College,* p. 13). See
Notes 11 and 12 below for studies of returning World War II
veterans and older students.

7. Jencks and Riesman, *The Academic Revolution,* p. 133.

8. See Note 2, above. For a psychological and sociological analysis
of the predisposition of many modern young people to postpone
commitment, see Joseph Katz et al., *No Time for Youth;* Kenneth
Keniston, *The Uncommitted;* Jack Douglas, *Youth in Turmoil;*
and Erik Erikson, *Identity. Youth and Crisis.*

9. Acceptance of the value and legitimacy of interrupting the
lockstep is becoming widespread. Some elite colleges, such as

Brown and Radcliffe, whose policies have national impact, accept students but defer their entry for a year to encourage broader experience. Beloit in Wisconsin goes further and provides special guidance during such a year for those students who want it. Harvard has instituted an Office of Career Services and Off-Campus Learning as an aid to the one undergraduate in five who takes out a year or more before completing his degree (a figure cited by Derek Bok in "The President's Report 1971–72"). Parents are reassured in the popular media that there can be valid reasons for "stopping out" and that 80% of those who drop out return to school (*Business Week,* April 21, 1973, p. 77). Noting the value of constructive work experience in focusing goals and interests, some institutions have integrated a program of work into their learning styles (examples include Antioch, Northeastern in Massachusetts, Drexel in Philadelphia, and Georgia Tech). The University Year for Action is a new incentive for this trend. For further discussion and proposals which encourage more such work opportunities for youth before or during college, see our paper *Report on Higher Education: The Federal Role: A GI Bill for Community Service.*

10. See, for example: Brent Breedin, "Veterans in College," which includes summaries of other studies; Norman Fredericksen and W. B. Schrader, *Adjustment to College: A Study of 10,000 Veteran and Non-Veteran Students in Sixteen American Colleges;* Harry Gideonse, "Educational Achievement of Veterans at Brooklyn College"; Keith Olson, "A Historical Analysis of the G.I. Bill and its Relationship to Higher Education"; John Paraskevopoulos and L. F. Robinson, "Comparison of College Performance of Cold War Veterans." The improved performance of students—including a group of veterans—who reentered the University of Utah after a period of absence is documented and discussed in L. Howard Campbell and Walter Hahn, "Readmission of Former Students After Absence from the Campus: Problems and Opportunities."

11. See Melissa Lewis Richter and Jan Banks Whipple, *A Revolution in the Education of Women: Ten Years of Continuing Education at Sarah Lawrence College,* pp. 34–41. For the experiment at the University of Texas, which consisted of admitting students

older than 25 without requiring SAT scores, see "College Finds Older Students Do Better," *Los Angeles Times,* April 6, 1973, and "Academic Status of Students 25 Years or Older Who Were Accepted to the University of Texas at Arlington Without the Admission Examination," unpublished paper, Arlington, Texas, summer 1973. See also the study by Campbell and Hahn, "Readmission of Former Students."

12. Fredericksen and Schrader (*Adjustment to College*) document the benefits of the age diversity on campus brought about by GIs.

13. See the Task Force paper *A GI Bill for Community Service.* A bill embodying some of these ideas has already been introduced by Congressman William Steiger (the "Community Service Fellowship Act," H.R. 17084).

14. There is considerable debate over how much diversity actually does exist. It is clear, on the one hand, that there has been a long-term trend toward institutional homogeneity, so that small institutions, sectarian institutions, single-sex institutions, and private colleges generally are educating a declining share of the population. (See Hodgkinson, *Institutions in Transition;* Jencks and Riesman, *The Academic Revolution,* Chapter 1; and Notes 7–9 in Chapter 4.) The resulting gap between the broad needs of contemporary students and the narrow traditional functions of higher education has been noted by Milton Schwebel in "Pluralism and Diversity in American Higher Education," and by Patricia Cross in *Beyond the Open Door,* p. 5. On the other hand, it is now clear that there is a significant trend toward diversity which aims at meeting new student needs and which is counteracting the homogenization of institutions. For examples and discussion see: Neal Berte, ed., *Innovations in Undergraduate Education: Selected Institutional Profiles and Thoughts about Experimentalism;* George Nolfi, *Selected Problems in Innovation in American Higher Education;* Carnegie Commission on Higher Education, *Reform on Campus: Changing Students, Changing Academic Programs;* Ann Heiss, *An Inventory of Academic Innovation and Reform;* Samuel B. Gould and K. Patricia Cross, eds., *Explorations in Non-Traditional Study;* Ohmer Milton, *Alternatives to*

the Traditional; and Diversity by Design, a report by the Commission on Non-Traditional Study. Recent examples of radically different institutions are described in a series of articles in Change, Vol. 1, No. 5, February 1972.

15. There is ample evidence that clear institutional objectives lead to a greater impact on students (see Arthur Chickering, Education and Identity, pp. 158–184). Well-established examples are Bennington College in Vermont, St. John's in Annapolis, and the Julliard School of the Performing Arts. Examples of less traditional, well-founded institutions are the University of Wisconsin at Green Bay, the College of Human Services, the John Jay College of Criminal Justice, and the Fashion Institute of Technology (the last three in New York City).

16. Alternative approaches to the traditional styles of education are being attempted, for example, at colleges like Empire State in New York and Minnesota Metro in St. Paul (which have incorporated the TV-correspondence format of Britain's Open University), Friend's World College (which incorporates travel as a learning experience), the New School of Social Research in New York (a flexible, interdisciplinary, individual study and project approach to professional education), Miami-Dade Junior College (an open-circuit TV external degree), Simon's Rock in Massachusetts (tutorial system and problem-solving orientation), Evergreen State College in Washington (a variety of learning modes in an approach to a broad theme which is emphasized for a semester or year), and the many institutions participating in the Union for Experimenting Colleges and Universities (each of which implements in a different way a variety of resources and styles of learning). A detailed description and classification of several hundred institutions manifesting new features can be found in Nolfi, Problems in Innovation. See also the sources listed in Note 14 above.

17. For recent recommendations for more flexible learning periods, see Carnegie Commission on Higher Education, Less Time, More Options. There is a striking lack of rationale (or cogent rationale) for many of the bureaucratic conventions characterizing American

higher education. The four-year degree is a good example, since the reasons for the widespread adoption of this model are not obvious. Jencks and Riesman write that, despite many nineteenth-century experiments to the contrary, most colleges had by World War I opted for a four-year baccalaureate (*The Academic Revolution,* p. 31). Edward Jones and Gloria Ortner (*College Credit by Examination*) identify the following influences which led to the formalization of college education into a four-year curriculum:

(1) There was little trust put in final examinations, and external examinations had no tradition in the United States. Hence, time spent on the college campus became a convenient measure.

(2) The accrediting agencies which started functioning in 1914, in seeking a standard by which to measure the colleges, promoted the theory that all students should take a prescribed amount of work in a prescribed fashion.

(3) State universities or education departments have been able to regularize college practices through their control of degrees and certificates.

(4) American educators came to emphasize four years of social and intellectual campus living, quite apart from credits earned.

(5) Preprofessional requirements tended to stipulate a four-year curriculum.

(6) Some institutions needed four years of tuition and dormitory fees for regular budgeting.

The credit hour system which came to be used to divide up the four-year curriculum into standardized units also rests on an arbitrary foundation. It derives from a 1906 decision by the Carnegie Commission for the Advancement of Teaching to use accumulated time in the classroom spent on a subject as the criterion for teacher retirement eligibility (Hannah Kreplin, *Credit by Examination,* p. 2).

18. For examples, see "Nontraditional Learning," in Warren Willingham, *The Source Book for Higher Education,* pp. 381–386. See also the sources cited in Note 14, above, and in Note 23, Chapter 1.

19. For a description of the history of recurrent education in Europe, see Herbert E. Striner, *Continuing Education as a National Capital Investment.* Striner provides detailed descriptions of re-

current education programs in Denmark, France, and Germany. See also Gruno Stein and S. M. Miller, "Recurrent Education: An Alternative System"; Dennis Kallen, "European Views on Recurrent Education"; and papers presented at the Organization for Economic Cooperation and Development's Conference on Recurrent Education held at Georgetown University in March 1973.

20. A discussion of the role of recurrent education in dealing with problems such as obsolescence and lack of career mobility can be found in Chapter 5 of *Work in America*. See also Charles E. Silberman, *The Myths of Automation,* and Edwin Mansfield, *The Economics of Technological Change,* Chapter 5.

21. See Vladimir Stoikov, "The Economics of Recurrent Education," a paper presented at the OECD Conference on Recurrent Education, Georgetown University, March 1973 (particularly p. 29).

22. For a discussion of "dead-end" jobs, career ladders, and proposals for redesigning jobs to deal with these problems, see *Work in America,* pp. 20, 32–34, 95, 121–126, and 140. Chapter 4 (pp. 93–120) of that report deals comprehensively with "The Redesign of Jobs."

Unfortunately, career mobility is often greatly hampered by unnecessary job requirements which usually involve credentials and which are all too often designed only to unjustly restrict entry to a profession. According to the 1973 *Manpower Report of the President,* "It is also evident that employment qualifications established by potential employers tend to rise with the increase in the qualifications of jobseekers. If most new entrants to the labor force can present credentials indicating the completion of 4 years of high school, the status of the high school dropout suffers by comparison, quite apart from the actual requirements of the job for which the applicant is being considered."

23. There are indications that various postsecondary education programs which have been treated as "second-class citizens" in the past are now being judged more fairly and given more credit for being educationally effective. Federal student aid provisions have been changed in recent years to allow for more aid to students

outside the traditional perimeters of higher education. Section 1202 of the Higher Education Amendments of 1972 gave a sizeable boost to the fortunes of proprietary institutions by mandating that representatives of proprietaries be included on the statewide co-ordinating commissions described in section 1202. The increasing usage of the term "postsecondary education" indicates that more and more people realize there is a much broader legitimate educational domain than that covered by the term "higher education" alone. The National Advisory Council on Vocational Education, established by Congress in 1968, said in a 1969 report that Americans in recent years have promoted the idea that "the only good education is an education capped by four years of college." The report branded this attitude as "snobbish, undemocratic and a revelation of why schools fail so many students." For more information on this report, see the *New York Times,* November 22, 1970.

24. See Fred Hechinger, "What 'Tearing Down the Walls' Can Do"; Alan Pifer, "Is it Time for an External Degree?"; Amiel T. Sharon, *College Credit for Off-Campus Study;* and John Valentine, *The External Degree.*

25. See Asa S. Knowles, ed., *Handbook of College and University Administration,* Vol. II, Sec. 5; John D. Krumboltz and Carl E. Thoresen, eds., *Behavioral Counseling: Cases and Techniques;* and Donald E. Super et al., *Computer-Assisted Counseling.*

26. Striner describes the French and German methods of financing recurrent education in great detail in *Continuing Education,* pp. 25, 26, 42–45, and 81–92.

27. See Striner, *Continuing Education,* pp. 61–65 and 71–74; and Frank Boddy, "Financial Options and Structural Requirements," a paper presented at the OECD Conference on Recurrent Education, Georgetown University, March 1973.

4. New Political Realities

1. Table A shows the growth of average campus size over a twenty-year period. Approximately 40.5% of all students were enrolled in

Table A. Percent Distribution of Institution Enrollments, 1950–1970

	≤ 1,000	1,000–4,999	5,000–9,999	≥ 10,000
1950	76	18	3	2
1960	63	28	5	4
1970	47	37	9	7

Source: *A Fact Book on Higher Education*, Third Issue, 1972, p. 72.123.

multicampus institutions in 1968, according to the Carnegie Commission on Higher Education report by Eugene C. Lee and Frank M. Bowen (*The Multicampus University*, p. xix). By 1967, there were 55 campuses with 20,000 or more students enrolled. These 55 campuses enrolled a total of 1,739,000 students, or 27% of total college enrollment. Two percent of the total number of institutions in the country enrolled 25% of the students. See Seymour E. Harris, *A Statistical Portrait of Higher Education,* pp. 385–387.

2. By April of 1972, over 70% of the faculty at more than 28% of the public two-year colleges were tenured. A similar trend of increasing percentages of tenured faculty is also occurring at four-year campuses. At the University of Colorado, officials have predicted that maintaining present practices will lead in five years to a faculty that is 90% tenured. See "Tenure for College Teachers Supported," *New York Times,* March 25, 1973. The figures on faculty age come from *Faculty Tenure,* p. 232.

3. Opening fall enrollment for 1972 was 9,204,156, compared to 9,025,032 in 1971, an increase of 1.9%. The average yearly increase during the 1950s was 4.6%. Between 1955 and 1960 the average increase was 6.5%, and during the 1960s it was 8.2%. Thus the percentage drop in the last few years is quite significant. These percentages were derived from opening fall enrollment figures in *A Fact Book on Higher Education,* First Issue, 1973, p. 73.9. Figures are not yet available for fall 1973 enrollment, but there are signs that the increase this year may be even smaller than last year. A survey of 109 major state university systems and campuses by the National Association of State Universities and Land Grant

Colleges found that applications for fall 1973 had decreased by 4.2% overall as compared with the figures for spring 1972. Last year the growth in applications was only 1.4%. (Reported in the *New York Times,* April 15, 1973.)

4. Between 1968 and 1973, federal funding for higher education grew from $5,204,000 to $7,400,000. See Figure 1 in Chapter 5, for a graph showing federal spending from 1938 to 1973, and see Note 11 of that chapter for information on the sources of the graph.

5. The last 50–50 enrollment split between public and private institutions occurred in 1951. In 1956 the split was 57% public and 43% private. (Source: *A Fact Book on Higher Education,* First Issue, 1973, p. 73.9.)

6. There are, for example, no private institutions in Wyoming. There is only one private institution in Nevada: Sierra Nevada College, which enrolls 99 people, or .6% of Nevada students. Only 10.4% of Alaska's students are enrolled in private institutions, 9.3% of Hawaii's, 9.1% of Montana's, 8% of New Mexico's, 6% of North Dakota's, and 2% of Arizona's. (Source: *Education Directory: Higher Education, 1972–73.*)

7. Northampton Junior College and Malcolm X Liberation University (Greensboro, N.C.) are the examples mentioned in the text. While the number of private colleges in 1972 (1,493) is larger than the number in 1965 (1,417), that number has grown by only 76 as against an increase of 403 in public institutions, from 790 in 1965 to 1,193 in 1972. (Source: *A Fact Book on Higher Education,* Third Issue, 1972, p. 72.117, and the *Education Directory, 1972–1973,* p. xxii.)

Particularly hard-hit have been women's colleges and Catholic colleges. Between 1960 and 1972, 152 of the 298 women's colleges either became coeducational or closed, according to a study by the Educational Testing Service's College Research Center ("Women's Schools Cut Back Since '60," *New York Times,* May 1, 1973). In 1960, according to the same study, three of every five women's colleges were under Roman Catholic auspices; in 1972 there were only 73 Catholic women's colleges remaining, 85 having become coeducational and 27 having closed. An article in the *National Catholic Reporter,* Kansas City, Mo. ("See Trouble for Catholic Colleges," August 4, 1972) states that since 1971, seven of the nation's 275 Catholic colleges have closed, and six have merged.

8. The merger of six Catholic colleges since 1971 was mentioned in Note 7. *The Chronicle of Higher Education* lists nine mergers that have either taken place or are planned for the period 1972–1975 ("College Openings and Closings," September 4, 1973). Mergers are, however, not solely a phenomenon of the private sector; in the 1971–72 academic year, the Wisconsin State Universities became part of the University of Wisconsin system, almost doubling the size of that system. See Note 10 of this chapter for a further discussion of the Wisconsin merger.

9. During the academic year 1957–58, tuition and required fees for a full-time undergraduate student in a public university averaged $205, and in a private university, $798, or 3.89 times as much. During academic 1969–70, the average cost at a private university was 4.47 times the cost at a public university ($1,795 as opposed to $402). (Source: *Basic Student Charges,* U.S. Office of Education, U.S. Government Printing Office, Washington, D.C.) Between the years 1960–61 and 1972–73, the basic costs of attending college rose by 68% for the average in-state student in residence at a public institution and by 94% for the comparable student at a private college or university. In real terms, the increases were 15% and 33% respectively (*Projections of Educational Statistics to 1980–81,* U.S. Office of Education, U.S. Government Printing Office, Washington, D.C., 1972, Tables 43, 44).

10. Eugene C. Lee and Frank M. Bowen (*The Multicampus University,* pp. 7–8) describe the state of multicampus universities in 1970. During that year, nine multicampus systems enrolled 900,000 students, or 17% of all students in public four-year colleges and universities. These nine systems awarded 25% of all bachelor's degrees given in public higher education for that year. And multicampus systems are proliferating; between 1968 and 1970, four new systems were created in Indiana, Nebraska, Massachusetts, and Tennessee. They also involve immense numbers of students. In the article "SUNY is No. 1 in Enrollment" (*Chronicle of Higher*

Education, January 3, 1972), full-time enrollment in the State University system of New York is given as 226,623. The second-largest system is that of the California State Colleges, enrolling 181,328 full-time students; third is the City University of New York, with 11,288; and fourth is the University of Wisconsin system, which almost doubled in size when the Wisconsin State Universities merged with the University of Wisconsin system, and which now enrolls 108,040 full-time students. For the past several years, the New York State Legislature has discussed the possibility of merging the SUNY and CUNY systems, which would result in a giant system enrolling about 600,000 part- and full-time students.

11. See Note 12 in Chapter 6. See also "Education Rivalry 's Worry to UT," *Knoxville (Tenn.) News Sentinel,* September 15, 1972, and "Politics, University Rivalries Shift Power to Illinois Board," *Chronicle of Higher Education,* October 30, 1972.

12. Officers of the multicampus systems head organizations so vast that it is hard to imagine how they could maintain close contact with students or even with individual campuses. Chancellor Ernest Boyer, for instance, presides over a network of more than 70 institutions in New York State. The professional staffs interposed between the officers and coordinating agencies of multicampus systems and the campuses are also very large. In California, the Board of Regents of the University of California has a professional staff of 433 individuals. The California State College Board of Trustees has a professional staff of 291, while the Board of Governors of the California Community Colleges has a staff of 98. The University of Tennessee trustees have a professional staff of 164 people, with a support staff of 168. (Statistics from the Governance Paper of this Task Force, to be released. Source: *Education Commission of the States.*)

13. See Lee and Bowen, *The Multicampus University,* and Bennis and Biederman, *The Leaning Ivory Tower.*

14. An example of a large and strong system-wide union is the Professional Staff Congress, which represents 16,000 professional employees in the City University of New York system. The PSC was formed in 1972 from a merger of the Legislative Conference

and the United Federation of College Teachers, previously the bargaining agents for CUNY faculty and staff. The PSC describes itself as the largest university union in the country. See "Faculty Members at City U Choose a Single Bargaining Agent," *New York Times,* June 8, 1972. For a discussion of the aims and methods of the PSC, see "CUNY Faculty Union Encounters Hard Bargaining," *Chronicle of Higher Education,* September 25, 1972.

15. Ever since collective bargaining became a force on campuses, there has been a continuing debate about the causes behind unionization. In *Governance of Higher Education: Six Priority Problems,* the Carnegie Commission cites six causes it views as central to the expansion of unionization. They are: "1) salaries are rising more slowly; real income, in some instances, has actually been reduced; 2) budgetary support for faculty interests is much harder to obtain; 3) more efforts are being made to control conditions of employment, such as workload; 4) students have intruded into what were once faculty preserves for decision-making, and these intrusions and their possible extension are a source of worry for many faculty members; 5) external authorities, outside the reach of faculty influence, are making more of the decisions that affect the campus and the faculty; 6) policies on promotion and tenure are more of an issue both as the rate of growth of higher education slows down, thus making fewer opportunities available, and as women and members of minority groups compete more actively for such opportunities as exist" (p. 39). See also: Robert Doherty, "The National Labor Relations Act and Higher Education: Prospects and Problems"; Robert A. Carr and Daniel K. Vaneyck, *Collective Bargaining Comes to the Campus;* Carol H. Shulman, *Collective Bargaining on Campus;* Gus Tyler, "The Faculty Joins the Proletariat"; and Kenneth S. Tollett, "The Faculty and the Government."

16. See Robert K. Carr and Daniel K. Vaneyck, *Collective Bargaining;* William Boyd, "Collective Bargaining in Academe: Causes and Consequences"; Donald Wollett, "The Status and Trend of Collective Negotiations for Faculty in Higher Education"; Kenneth S. Tollett, "Faculty and Government"; and Robert E. Doherty, "NLRA and Higher Education."

17. A classic example of attempts at greater outside control of campus life came during a recess at a 1968 New York State Legislature hearing on student disciplinary policies at the Stony Brook campus of the State University of New York. During that recess, a senator approached a Stony Brook administrator and said, "You people out there don't believe in *in loco parentis,* do you?" The administrator replied, "No, I guess we don't." The senator then commented, "Well, you darn well will believe in it when we get through with you." (Reported in the *Chronicle of Higher Education,* March 3, 1968.) For details on faculty workload legislation, see Note 2, Chapter 6.

18. All too often, federal programs for the sake of organizational convenience, have helped accelerate the trend to central control by funneling student or institutional funding through coordinating agencies. Some educators fear that the 1202 commissions mandated in the Higher Education Amendments of 1972 will exacerbate this problem. See "U.S. Involvement in State Planning Alarms Colleges," *Chronicle of Higher Education,* December 18, 1972. For further evidence of this trend to centralized control, see *Statewide Planning for Postsecondary Education,* pp. 35–37. For a discussion of the 1202 commissions, see Note 14, Chapter 6.

19. For a discussion of the causes of the proliferation of credentials and alternatives to credentialism, see S. M. Miller, "Strategies for Reducing Credentialism," *ACTION,* Summer 1970. Information on studies of the relationship between education and credentials and job performance is given by Ivar Berg in *Education and Jobs: The Great Training Robbery.*

20. Examples taken from Myron Lieberman, *Tyranny of the Experts.*

21. *Report on Licensure and Related Health Personnel Credentialing,* p. 47.

22. See Lieberman, *Tyranny of Experts,* for a discussion of professional groups' control of educating programs.

23. *Report on Licensure and Related Health Personnel Credentialing,* p. 214. The Board of Registry of Medical Technologists is part of the American Society of Clinical Pathologists.

24. See *Nationally Recognized Accrediting Agencies and Associations,* U.S. Department of Health, Education, and Welfare, Accreditation and Institutional Eligibility Staff, Washington, D.C., March 1972.

25. See "Minimum Requirements for Admission to Legal Practice in the U.S.," *Review of Legal Education,* 1969.

26. For a list of accrediting agencies, see *Nationally Recognized Accrediting Agencies and Associations.*

5. The Federal Presence in Higher Education

1. A number of federal commissions have been charged with the study of policy for education beyond high school (see Charles A. Quattlebaum, *Federal Educational Policies, Programs and Proposals,* Part I, pp. 69–98, and Alice Rivlin, *The Role of the Federal Government in Financing Higher Education,* pp. 20–23). Yet the first serious debate within the government over federal programs occurred only in 1972, over the Educational Amendments. Even then, the debate was fragmentary and did not address the GI Bill, Social Security benefits, or graduate student aid, since these topics did not fall within specific committee responsibility.

2. See Rivlin, *Role of the Federal Government,* pp. 9–13, and John J. Whealen, *A History of Federal Aid to Education, 1785–1965,* p. 11. Aid from the colonies for private institutions in the form of funds, land grants, state-authorized lotteries, and tax exemption preceded federal aid (see Carnegie Commission on Higher Education, *The Capitol and the Campus,* pp. 11–14).

3. Although the Morrill Act (1862) was clearly instrumental in legitimizing nonclassical studies in agriculture, engineering, and other practical subjects, and in broadening access to provide for the practical training of women and the offspring of industrial and farm workers, the extent to which the rhetoric of land-grant reform was actually translated into reality has been questioned. From a review of primary sources for the period 1870–90, Peter Fitzgerald concludes that, at the two land-grant universities of Illinois and Minnesota, the ideals of land-grant reform received

but cursory implementation, as evidenced by the composition of the student bodies, faculties, boards of trustees, and curricula of these institutions (*Democracy, Utility and Two Land-Grant Colleges in the Nineteenth Century: The Rhetoric and the Reality of Reform*). Despite this evidence, the long-term effects of the land-grant philosophy on the functions and forms of higher education remain substantiated. See, for example, Rivlin, *Role of the Federal Government,* pp. 9–23.

4. Relying on data from the U.S. Office of Education, June O'Neill shows peak federal funding prior to 1940 as $43.2 million in 1935–36 (*Sources of Funds to Colleges and Universities,* Table A-1, p. 28).

5. *Statistical Abstract of the United States,* U.S. Department of Commerce, Bureau of the Census, Washington, D.C., 1945.

6. See Figure 1. An interesting illustration of this was noted by William G. Bowen in his 1969 testimony to the Joint Economic Committee of Congress: Chicago, Princeton, and Vanderbilt averaged only 1.4% of their budgets from government grants and contracts in 1939–40, but 45.9% in 1965–66. (Cited in *Tax Reform and the Crisis of Financing Higher Education,* p. iv.)

7. Information obtained from yet unpublished data of the National Commission for the Financing of Post-Secondary Education.

8. The most recent instance of federal support of an area of new interest is President Nixon's proposal for a five-year, $10 billion research program in energy as a part of a broad national program to meet the energy crisis.

9. Calculated from: June O'Neill, *Sources of Funds,* pp. 28–29, and U.S. Bureau of the Census, *Statistical Abstract of the United States* (93rd edition), Washington, D.C., 1972, p. 312. Note that these expenditures were for *higher* education, not for the remainder of postsecondary education, which has benefited less from federal funding.

10. *National Patterns of Research and Development Resources, 1953–1971,* pp. 15–18. For the background to federal involvement in academic science, see Vannevar Bush, *Science, the Endless Fron-*

tier. For later developments, see J. Stefan Dupree and Sanford A. Lakoff, *Science and the Nation.*

11. Early postwar decisions established a dual path for research sponsorship: the military agencies, having learned the importance of science, were determined to continue a close coupling with research, while there was at the same time a strong sense in the Congress, the Administration, and the universities that much research ought to be through civilian federal sponsorship—a concern reflected in the debate over civilian control of the Atomic Energy Commission in 1946 and the establishment of the National Science Foundation in 1950.

12. Figures 1, 4, 5, and 6 were constructed from data derived from diverse and often conflicting sources (see Table A). They should, however, provide a reasonable though rough picture of trends in federal funding.

Table A. Federal Resources for Higher Education by Program Type, Selected Fiscal Years 1938–1973 (millions of dollars)

	Institutional Grants	Facilities and Equipment	Student Support	Veterans Education[a]*	Research and Development	Total
1938	10.53	22.81	10.54	—	6.2	50.0
1947	28.63	1.37	—	1,000.0	150.0	1,180.0
1952	45.11	2.29	4.37	365.7	220.0	638.4
1957	70.90	129.80	7.75	454.9	229.0	892.3
1963	163.08	349.19	199.13	44.8	760.0	1,516.0
1968	1,142.72	981.77	1,183.91	334.9	1,450.0	5,093.3
1973*	1,405.91	314.42	2,141.00	1,849.2	1,802.0	7,512.5

* Estimated

a. For 1952–1973, figures represent V.A. estimates of direct benefits to veterans in colleges and universities only. The 1947 figure is an extrapolation based on V.A. figures.

For 1938 through 1963, figures represent obligations; thereafter, they represent expenditures. However, where obligations would be a poor proxy for expenditures (e.g., 1963 construction grants) and the amounts involved are relatively large, we have generally substituted expenditures. Primary sources were: *Social Welfare Expenditures Under Public Programs in the United States, 1929–66; Special Analyses. Budget of the United States Government, Fiscal Years 1967–73; National Patterns of Research and Development Resources, 1953–1971.*

"Student Aid" includes undergraduate and graduate grants, fellowships, traineeships, and support for teacher training. "Research and Development" excludes monies for federally funded research and development centers associated with colleges and universities.

13. Figures 2 and 3 were constructed from data obtained in a personal communication with the National Science Foundation.

14. The concentration of research funds in relatively few universities is striking, though it has decreased slightly in the past decade: in Fiscal Year 1963, the top 100 recipients of research monies took 90% of the total; in 1967 they received 88% and in 1971 and 1972, 86%. The top 10 institutions received 34% in 1963, 29% in 1967, and 27% in 1971, even though they represent less than 2% of all recipients of federal research grants and less than 1½% of all universities and colleges (*Federal Support to Universities, Colleges, and Selected Non-Profit Institutions, Fiscal Year 1971,* p. 11).

15. The National Youth Administration coordinated a college student work program from 1935 to 1943, serving an estimated 800,-000 students. See Rivlin, *Role of the Federal Government,* pp. 63–64, and Quattlebaum, *Federal Educational Policies,* Part I, pp. 20–21.

16. See Rivlin, *Role of the Federal Government,* p. 67.

17. Doctoral candidates supported by federal fellowships comprised only a few percent in 1950, rose to 17% by 1968, and fell back to 12% by 1970 (*Report on Federal Postdoctoral Support, Part I, Fellowships and Traineeships,* Appendix C, Tables 1–10).

18. Work-study funds were legislated in 1964 (Quattlebaum, *Fed-*

eral Educational Policies, Part II, p. 202), Educational Opportunity Grants and Social Security Student Benefits in 1965 (ibid., p. 208 and p. 251).

19. *Special Analysis. Budget of the United States Government,* Fiscal Year 1974.

20. Although the Public Works Administration (and the Works Progress Administration) programs were not primarily designed to aid higher education, they did contribute significantly to the construction of facilities in public colleges and universities. By 1939 almost $200,000 had been loaned under PWA College Building Projects. In addition, many campuses profited from war surplus (including whole army camps, transported to campus). For a description of these programs, see Rivlin, *Role of the Federal Government,* pp. 98–100, and Wolk, *Alternative Methods of Federal Funding for Higher Education.*

21. See Rivlin, *Role of the Federal Government,* pp. 100–105, and Wolk, *Alternative Methods of Funding,* p. 15.

22. In 1956, the Health Research Facilities Act authorized the first grants ($90 million) for laboratories; then, in 1960, the National Science Foundation started to subsidize graduate-level research facilities in engineering and science. The estimated annual need for an additional $1 billion for academic facilities led in 1963 to the Higher Education Facilities Act, which provided $1/3$ matching grants for undergraduate facilities, and, by amendment in 1966, grants for graduate construction, loans for almost any four-year college facilities, and an annual allocation for community colleges. See Wolk, *Alternative Methods of Funding,* pp. 17–22, and Froomkin, *Students and Buildings,* pp. 29–31.

23. Wolk, *Alternative Methods of Funding,* p. 18.

24. West Point was founded in 1802 and Howard in 1867. See Rivlin, *Role of the Federal Government,* pp. 108–115.

25. In 1961 appropriations from the second Morrill Act amounted to about $5 million (Rivlin, *Role of the Federal Government,* p. 20); in 1962 they totaled $10.7 million (*Fact Book,* Bureau of Higher Education, Office of Education, United States

Department of Health, Education, and Welfare, Washington, D.C., 1971); and in 1968 they totaled $14.5 million (*Toward a Long-Range Plan for Federal Support for Higher Education,* Table A-4, p. 48). For a discussion of the roots of institutional aid, and the advantages and disadvantages of this approach, see Rivlin, *Role of the Federal Government,* pp. 9–23 and pp. 158–167.

26. Institutional aid was generated by the National Defense Education Act in 1958 (in the form of a supplement to balance tuition and educational costs incurred by the institution), and came from the National Science Foundation beginning in 1960, and the National Institutes of Health, beginning in 1961 (Wolk, *Alternative Methods of Funding,* pp. 31–33).

27. The 1972 Amendments include a program of aid to institutions based on a three-part formula: (1) 45% of the funds appropriated would be distributed according to the total amount of educational opportunity grants, work-study, and National Defense Loans paid to students at each college; (2) another 45% of the appropriation would be distributed according to the number of students at each institution receiving aid from the new "BEOGs" program; and (3) 10% of the aid would be based on the number of graduate students enrolled at each institution.

The provision for "bailing out" colleges and universities in the 1972 Amendments is perhaps the clearest example of a concern for institutions as institutions. Emergency assistance for institutions in financial distress would be available on grounds that "the Nation's institutions of higher education constitute a national resource which significantly contributes to the security, general welfare, and economy of the United States" (Sec. 122 [a] [1] [A], Title III, Education Amendments of 1972). Such measures and the general formula support which was also authorized would climax the evolution from special purpose support to general institutional aid.

28. In 1970–71, $1,503,800,000 was volunteered for the support of the 1,080 institutions of higher education surveyed by the Council for Financial Aid to Education, from which it is estimated that $1.86 billion was contributed to all American colleges and universities in that year (*Voluntary Support of Education, 1970–71;*

cited in *Tax Reform and the Crisis of Financing Higher Education,* p. 6).

29. Parents may claim a student as an exemption if they provide half the student's support. The student may claim an exemption as well (see Wolk, *Alternative Methods of Funding,* p. 36). Recently the IRS granted deductions for moving expenses for educational purposes.

30. At least three proposals which have been considered by the House Ways and Means Committee would diminish contributions to higher education: (1) taxation of gifts of appreciated assets; (2) limitation of the estate tax deduction for charitable gifts to 50% of the adjusted gross estate; and (3) the establishment of a "minimum taxable income" which would limit to one-half the portion of an individual's income that could be offset by the combination of exclusions and itemized deductions.

31. The federal government reviews the standards and procedures of accrediting agencies in determining the eligibility of institutions for federal funds, thereby extending federal sanction to these standards. See the forthcoming Task Force Paper on accreditation and institutional eligibility.

32. Affirmative Action requirements were legislated in Titles IV and VI of the 1965 Civil Rights Act, and Title IX of the 1972 Educational Amendments. The Director of the Office of Civil Rights once pointed out to the Task Force that he was the only one in the federal government who could shut off *all* federal funds to a university. Despite the admirable goals of the office, this is a troubling power.

33. The Cost Accounting Standards Board, created in 1970, has tended to pressure universities to adopt uniform accounting practices based on those used by industry, which could affect the organizational character of the institution. For example, at one point the Board proposed the establishment of individual cost center overhead rates which, rather than encouraging the profit center approach as in industry, might instead have prompted principal investigators to seek out low-overhead departments and push for separate administrative units.

34. Emergency assistance for institutions, for which funds were authorized in the Higher Education Amendments of 1972, have yet to be appropriated. If funds are appropriated, they will be allocated on the basis of a strikingly elaborate and detailed process of review and control of college financial plans (P.L. 92–318, Sec. 122[a] [2] [C]):

An application shall be approved under this subsection only if it includes such information, terms, and conditions as the Commissioner finds necessary and reasonable to enable him to carry out his functions under this section, and as he determines will be in the financial interest of the United States, and the applicant agrees—

(i) to disclose such financial information as the Commissioner determines to be necessary to determine the sources or causes of its financial distress and other information relating to its use of its financial resources;

(ii) to conduct a comprehensive cost analysis study of its operation, including income-cost comparisons and cost per credit hour of instruction for each department, in accordance with uniform standards prescribed by the Commissioner; and

(iii) to consider, and either implement or give adequate reasons in writing for not doing so, any financial or operational reform recommended by the Commissioner for the improvement of its financial condition.

35. The Environmental Protection Agency and the Justice Department have in the past attached to research grants publication restrictions which give those agencies the final decision as to whether a study is published or not. This type of regulation often conflicts with a university's policy of freedom to publish, and also conflicts with the Freedom of Information Act.

36. Many NASA, DOD, and NSF appropriation bills have had "antiriot riders" attached to them which forbid federal assistance in the form of loans, work-study, educational opportunity grants, or salary (often for two years) to any student or employee of an institution of higher education who (in the language of the often imitated Section 504 of the 1968 Higher Education Amendments, P.L. 90–575):

has been convicted by any court of record of any crime which was committed after the date of enactment of this Act and which involved the use (or assistance to others in the use of) force, disruption, or the seizure of property under control of any institution of higher education to prevent officials or students in such institution from engaging in their duties or pursuing their studies . . . [if] such crime was of a serious nature and contributed to a substantial disruption of the administration of the institution.

37. This proposal, which would have affected at least 15 major universities and colleges, was part of the Hebert Amendment to the 1972 House Armed Services Bill. The amendment was not included in the final act, but proponents of the original amendment have recently expressed the intention of sponsoring similar legislation in the future.

38. A "policy statement concerning students on boards of trustees" was adopted as a "sense of the Congress" resolution in the Educational Amendments of 1972 (P.L. 92–318).

39. H.R. 7248 would award two-thirds of institutional aid on the basis of full-time equivalent enrollment at institutions of higher education, which means prescribing "(1) the number of earned credits which constitute enrollment on a full-time basis, and (2) a definition of 'credit' to be used for such determinations which will be substantially uniform for all institutions" (Sec. 1203 [a] [5]). This would probably mean credit proliferation and the standardization of what constitutes a worthwhile academic experience, explicitly involving the federal government in the internal life of academic institutions.

40. Since June of 1970, when the National Labor Relations Board took jurisdiction of a case at Cornell on grounds that a private university of such size had substantial impact on interstate commerce, institutions of private higher education have been treated like private corporations. For several years there has been a general tendency for states to make provisions for collective bargaining by public employees; consequently, faculty at public institutions have been organizing. (Information given by Philip Semas of the *Chronicle of Higher Education*.)

41. Section 1202 of the Higher Education Amendments of 1972 requires states to establish planning commissions in order to receive certain federal funds. See Cheryl M. Fields, "U.S. Involvement in State Planning Alarms Colleges," *Chronicle of Higher*

Education, Dec. 18, 1972, p. 1. See also Chapter 6 and, especially, Note 14 in that chapter.

6. The Federal Role in Postsecondary Education

1. For a good general discussion of forces impinging on decision-making, see John Millett, *Decisionmaking and Administration in Higher Education.* The "balance of forces" concept is discussed in Chapter 7 of *Statewide Planning for Postsecondary Education* (see especially pp. 103–104 and 109–112). For a discussion of the faculty's role in decision-making, see *Faculty Participation in Academic Governance.*

2. As of January 1972, there were at least four states which had enacted legislation on faculty teaching workloads—Michigan, Texas, Washington, and Florida. A similar bill in New York was vetoed by Governor Rockefeller in 1971. The Florida law, for example, "requires full-time teaching faculty members to teach a minimum of 12 classroom contact hours per week." According to *Higher Education in the States,* "The legislature indicated that it is unwilling to continue to fund research at the current level and that it desires faculty members to increase their teaching in relation to research and other activities. It therefore set forth specifically in the appropriations bill a section that provided that teaching productivity and skills shall be the principal factors in granting tenure or continuing the employment of instructional personnel and prohibiting against denying tenure, promotion, or continued employment solely on the basis of failure to publish. The legislature further emphasized its desire to see an increase in teaching productivity by directly addressing and proscribing the right to limit enrollment at the upper division, and by increasing teacher productivity by about 4% in terms of student credit hours." (*Higher Education in the States,* October 1971).

Teaching load legislation usually includes arbitrary formulas which attempt to quantify academic judgments. The Texas legislation, for example, mandates that classes containing more than 100 students, but less than 300 students, will count as one and one-half courses. Classes containing 300 or more students count as two classes. This approach continues throughout the bill with such subsections as "chairmanship of three doctoral student (or five masters student) committees shall be the equivalent of one course for a maximum of three years (or two years in the case of masters students)."

For faculty reaction to these laws, see "Faculty Dissatisfaction Widespread at U. of Texas, Many Charge Political Maneuvering by Regents," *Chronicle of Higher Education*, May 22, 1972.

3. A concise, yet comprehensive, view of accountability in higher education can be found in Kenneth Mortimer, *Accountability in Higher Education*. Chapter 3 provides an especially good overview of external accountability, especially accountability as interpreted by governmental agencies. Robert M. O'Neil in *The Courts, Government and Higher Education,* describes how people have increasingly turned to the courts and other regulatory agencies in attempts to force institutions of higher education to conform to their concepts of accountability. The scenario of rapidly expanding litigation which O'Neil describes could easily apply to many other fields as well.

4. Sometimes this is a result of the failure of the public agencies to understand the extent to which public needs are being met. For example, the attitude of many agencies towards faculty members' work loads and habits focuses on the few who are taking advantage of the system, not the efforts of most.

5. Frank Patterson, in *The Consortia: Interinstitutional Cooperation in American Higher Education* (unpublished draft), outlines the consortia movement, provides specific case studies and assesses the strengths, weaknesses, and possible future directions for consortia. Patterson identifies more than 60 consortia and provides an extensive bibliography. According to Patterson, "The performance of consortia up to this point has not measured well against the real opportunities and needs that have existed in American higher education in the past several decades. The general failure of the moment to deliver significant academic complementarity, or significant planned cooperation in capital outlay, or significant attention to operating economies that might be achieved through cooperation, or any substantial long-range planning of change and

development—together with the continuing preeminence of institutional autonomy regardless of the redundancy of results—reflects a major opportunity thus far lost by consortia in terms of higher education as it has been."

See also *Five College Cooperation: Directions for the Future; Expanding Opportunities: Case Studies of Interinstitutional Cooperation;* and Winfred L. Godwin, "Interinstitutional and Interstate Cooperation in American Higher Education."

6. The economy of scale issue is treated in great detail in James Maynard, *Some Microeconomics of Higher Education—Economies of Scale.* According to Maynard, "4-year colleges experience declining per-student costs until 5,363 FTE students are enrolled . . . The private schools usually are simply too small to enjoy the economies of scale realized by the large public institutions" (pp. 117 and 123). Discussing the cost inefficiency of institutions with enrollments far above and below the least-cost enrollment of 5,363, Maynard says: "The obvious answer is to channel additional students into the smaller schools, public or private, bringing them to efficient size and, perhaps, pursuing positive policies to reduce gradually the size of the 'multiversities'."

A good example of the magnitude of home office operations can be found by looking at the State University of New York (SUNY). In the fall of 1972, SUNY had an enrollment of 364,802 students at 72 campuses. Their central office had a staff of 427 people and an annual budget of approximately $7.6 million. This information came in an October 1973 phone conversation with Harry Charlton at the SUNY central office in Albany, New York.

7. See Eric Ashby, *Any Person, Any Study.* Ashby cites a study made by the Bureau of Social Research at Columbia which estimated that 15% of students on American campuses are there against their own will. Ashby also discusses high attrition rates and says, "when half of those entering higher education leave it without any certificate of competence, an observer is tempted to ask whether this does not represent an enormous undisclosed prodigality of resources . . . American society may not be affluent enough to allow this privilege in higher education in the 1980's. It may then become unrealistic, politically too, to spend millions

of dollars on places in college occupied by persons who are not gifted enough, or do not have the motivation, to benefit from the education which college provides."

8. Forcing private institutions to carry out certain orders should not be a part of state planning. Rather, state planners can work effectively *with* private institutions that are determining their own directions, and this will help keep public systems competitive. Some private institutions are transtate, even transnational and that is helpful.

9. Santa Cruz (Calif.), Evergreen (Wash.), Empire State (N.Y.), Minnesota Metro (Minn.), Sangamon (Ill.), and New College (Ala.) are all examples of new and innovative institutions which have been established in the public sector. See Ann Heiss, *An Inventory of Academic Innovation and Reform,* for small, but valuable profiles of many of the innovative institutions which have emerged in recent years. Even a cursory glance at the Heiss work will show that countless innovative institutions and procedural innovations have been established in the public sector in recent years.

10. See Notes 14, 16, 17, and 18 in Chapter 4.

11. The bases for student selection of institutions and programs are extremely complex. Often, of course, reasons for choosing a college are largely practical (proximity and cost) or somewhat arbitrary (advice of others, peer popularity). The choices are also likely to be further biased by information from counselors who are often not well-informed, and by images of institutions which are incomplete or false as a result of the manner in which colleges present themselves (see Kenneth Feldman and Theodore Newcomb, *The Impact of College on Students,* pp. 110–114, for a discussion of factors influencing student selection of college). Nonetheless, there is evidence that students to some degree select themselves into colleges and areas of study suited to their needs and aspirations. Arthur Chickering has shown that institutions with well-defined objectives attract students who share those goals, and that similar institutions attract similar students (*Education and Identity,* pp. 158–184).

    Within institutions, students tend to select fields on the basis of aspirations which reflect their own values, attitudes, and personality characteristics, which in turn show similarity to those of other students in the same field (Feldman and Newcomb, *Impact of College,* pp. 151–195). A study which solicited retrospective student assessment of the adequacy of the information on which their career choices were based found that over 60% thought the information satisfactory, with only about 18% regarding it as definitely inadequate. These students also had accurate perceptions of the labor market conditions prevailing in the main professions (Richard Freedman, *The Market for College-Trained Manpower,* pp. 194–200).

At the graduate level, there are several indices of sound student choice. NSF fellows, free to choose any university, concentrated themselves in a small number of excellent institutions (Alice Rivlin, *The Role of the Federal Government in Financing Higher Education,* p. 93). And students seem to have accurate assessments of market opportunities for specialized doctorate careers (Freedman, *Market for Manpower,* p. 200). For further discussion and evidence for the wisdom of student choice, see Alexander Astin and Robert C. Nichols, "Progress of the Merit Scholar: An Eight Year Follow-Up," and Theodore W. Schultz, "Resources for Higher Education: An Economist's View."

12. All institutions should compete and be judged on the basis of their educational effectiveness and not their political leverage. A vivid example of the wrong kind of competition, that which is based on political muscle, was seen in the recent efforts of the large public institutions in the state of Washington to have the state legislature end the life of a new experimental campus, Evergreen State, that was effective in attracting student applications at a time when applications were down at their institutions.

13. Student-based funding provides the federal government with a very good vehicle for preserving openness and fluidity in American postsecondary education. We believe that the GI Bill provided vivid proof of the fact that students are capable of making intelligent decisions about their education, based on educational effectiveness, and that federal student-based funding can be a major force for support of institutions based on their educational

effectiveness and not their political power. The Fund for the Improvement of Postsecondary Education (FIPSE) offers another fine opportunity for the federal government to be a force for diversity and innovation, which are key components of an open and fluid system of postsecondary education.

Some people feel that the ever growing multicampus systems are driving private colleges and universities out of business and are thus reducing competition. Some believe the federal government should bring antitrust action against some of these multicampus systems, but state exemptions from antitrust regulation make direct antitrust action unlikely. Others feel that antitrust suits should be brought against accrediting agencies for similar reasons and one proprietary institution has done so. In that case a district court judge ruled that the association was guilty of improper restraint of trade, but the decision was overturned on appeal. However, the appellate judge indicated that there could be situations in which an accreditation association could be exercising monopolistic power in violation of antitrust laws. See *Marjorie Webster Junior College v. Middle States Association of Colleges and Secondary Schools, Inc.,* No. 23351, U.S. Court of Appeals, Washington, D.C., June 30, 1970.

14. Section 1201, subsection a, of the Higher Education Amendments of 1972 reads:

Any state which desires to receive assistance under section 1203 or Title X shall establish a State Commission or designate an existing state agency or state commission (to be known as the State Commission) which is broadly and equitably representative of the general public and public and private nonprofit and proprietary institutions of postsecondary education in the State including community colleges (as defined in Title X), junior colleges, postsecondary vocational schools, area vocational schools, technical institutes, four-year institutions of higher education and branches thereof.

Section 1203, subsection a, of these amendments reads:

The Commissioner is authorized to make grants to any State Commission established pursuant to section 1202(a) to enable it to expand the scope of the studies and planning in Title X through comprehensive inventories of, and studies with respect to, all public and private postsecondary educational resources in the State, including planning necessary for such resources to be better coordinated, improved, expanded or altered so that all persons within the State who desire, and who can benefit from postsecondary education may have an opportunity to do so.

15. In 1970, the Office of Education published a series of pamphlets describing the 31 most successful compensatory education programs selected in a nationwide evaluation of projects by the American Institutes for Research. One booklet in the series describes each project's program activities, staffing, and budget: *It Works Series: Summaries of Selected Compensatory Education Projects*.

16. See *Federal Agencies and Black Colleges—Fiscal 1970;* and Charles A. Quattlebaum, *Federal Education Policies, Programs and Proposals,* Part 2, p. 202.

17. For examples of mission-focused colleges which aim at specific student needs and interests, see Note 15 to Chapter 3.

18. For examples of colleges with an ethnic focus, see Note 13 to Chapter 1.

19. The National Institute of Education has made 206 awards this year to researchers in elementary, secondary, and higher education, for a total of $11.3 million in grants. The Fund for the Improvement of Postsecondary Education has currently approved 89 grants totaling $9.3 million in its first series of research awards. See *Chronicle of Higher Education,* July 30, 1973.

20. See *Scientific American,* October 1972, for a detailed look at a negative income tax experiment which was carried out in five Pennsylvania and New Jersey cities beginning in 1968. The experiment is a perfect example of trying out a concept on a small scale before any possible implementation on a national basis.

21. See Note 3 to Chapter 6.

22. The GI Bill is the most obvious example of a federal higher education program with major but almost completely unforeseen consequences. Similarly, the decision to extend the jurisdiction of the National Labor Relations Board to encompass institutions of higher education (see Note 40 to Chapter 5) has had an impact considerably greater than initially expected. The 1202 guidelines

established by the higher education amendments of 1972 have had a far-reaching impact on the structure of state governance of post-secondary education (see Note 18 to Chapter 4). In California, a law creating a committee for postsecondary education was passed *in anticipation* of the 1202 regulations. There has also been a tendency to continue programs even when their influence is negative, because of a lack of careful analysis. A provision in the National Defense Education Act, which allows for reduced or eliminated repayment if the student becomes a teacher, was continued despite an obvious oversupply of teachers. Weak data-keeping and analysis have clearly inhibited federal leadership.

Bibliography

General

Ashby, Eric. *Any Person, Any Study: An Essay on American Higher Education,* The Carnegie Commission on Higher Education, McGraw-Hill, New York, 1971.

Bayer, Alan E., John K. Folger, and Helen S. Astin. *Human Resources and Higher Education,* Russell Sage Foundation, New York, 1970.

Berg, Ivar. *Education and Jobs: The Great Training Robbery,* Praeger, New York, 1970.

Blaug, Mark. *An Introduction to the Economics of Education,* Penguin Books, Middlesex, England, 1970.

Bowen, Howard R., and Paul Servelle. *Who Benefits from Higher Education—and Who Should Pay?* American Association for Higher Education, Washington, D.C., 1972.

Carnegie Commission on Higher Education. *Higher Education: Who Pays? Who Benefits? Who Should Pay?* McGraw-Hill, New York, 1973.

————. *The Purposes and the Performance of Higher Education in the United States Approaching the Year 2000,* McGraw-Hill, New York, 1973.

Carnoy, Martin, ed. *Schooling in a Corporate Society,* David McKay Company, New York, 1972.

Chickering, Arthur W. *Education and Identity,* Jossey-Bass, San Francisco, 1972.

Cross, K. Patricia. *Beyond the Open Door,* Jossey-Bass, San Francisco, 1971.

————. *New Students and New Needs in Higher Education,* Center for Research and Development in Higher Education, Berkeley, 1972.

Digest of Educational Statistics, 1968, 1969, 1970, 1971, 1972, U.S. Department of Health, Education, and Welfare, Office of Education, Washington, D.C., 1968–72.

Dressel, Paul L., et al. *Institutional Research in the University,* Jossey-Bass, San Francisco, 1971.

The Economics and Financing of Higher Education in the United States, A Compendium of Papers Submitted to the Joint Economic Committee, Congress of the United States, 91st Congress, 1st Session, U.S. Government Printing Office, Washington, D.C., 1969.

Education in the Seventies, U.S. Department of Health, Education, and Welfare, Office of Education, Washington, D.C., 1968.

A Fact Book on Higher Education, American Council on Education, Washington, D.C., annual supplements, 1969–1973.

Feldman, Kenneth A., and Theodore M. Newcomb. *The Impact of College on Students,* 2 vols., Jossey-Bass, San Francisco, 1969.

Harris, Seymour E. *A Statistical Portrait of Higher Education,* Carnegie Commission on Higher Education, McGraw-Hill, New York, 1972.

Hefferlin, J. G. Lon. *Dynamics of Academic Reform,* Jossey-Bass, San Francisco, 1971.

Hefferlin, J. G. Lon, Melvin J. Bloom, Jerry G. Gaff, and Brenda Jo Longacre. *Inventory of Current Research on Postsecondary Education,* Center for Research and Development in Higher Education, University of California, Berkeley, 1969.

Higher Education: Proposals by the Swedish 1968 Educational Commission, Stockholm, 1973.

Hodgkinson, Harold L. *Institutions in Transition: A Study of Change in Higher Education,* The Carnegie Commission on Higher Education, McGraw-Hill, New York, 1970.

Jencks, Christopher, and David Riesman. *The Academic Revolution,* Doubleday & Co., Garden City, N.Y., 1968.

Jerome, Judson. *Culture Out of Anarchy: The Reconstruction of American Higher Learning,* Herder and Herder, New York, 1971.

Ladd, Dwight R. *Change in Educational Policy: Self-Studies in Selected Colleges and Universities,* Carnegie Commission on Higher Education, McGraw-Hill, New York, 1970.

Lambert, Richard D., ed. *American Higher Education: Prospects and Choices,* The Annals of the American Academy of Political and Social Science, Philadelphia, 1972.

The Learning Society. Report of the Commission on Post-Secondary Education in Ontario, Ministry of Government Services, Toronto, 1972.

Mayhew, Lewis B. *The Literature of Higher Education 1972,* Jossey-Bass, San Francisco, 1972.

Perry, William G., Jr. *Forms of Intellectual and Ethical Development in College Years,* Holt, Rinehart and Winston, New York, 1970.

Priorities in Higher Education, Report of the President's Task Force on Higher Education (Hester Commission), Washington, D.C., 1970.

Projections of Education Statistics to 1977–78, U.S. Department of Health, Education, and Welfare, Office of Education, Washington, D.C., 1969.

Rawls, John. *A Theory of Justice,* Harvard University Press, Cambridge, Mass., 1971.

Snyder, Benson R. *The Hidden Curriculum,* A. A. Knopf, New York, 1971.

Special Analyses. Budget of the United States Government, Fiscal Years 1968–1974, U.S. Government Printing Office, Washington, D.C., annual issues, 1967–1973.

Study of Education at Stanford, The Steering Committee of the Study of Education at Stanford, Stanford University, Stanford, Calif., November 1968 et seq.

Toward Balanced Growth: Quantity with Quality, Report of the National Goals Research Staff, The White House, Washington, D.C., 1970.

Tyack, David B., ed. *Turning Points in American Educational History,* Blaisdell Publishing Co., Waltham, Mass., 1967.

Veysey, Laurence R. *The Emergence of the American University,* University of Chicago Press, Chicago, 1965.

Whitehead, Alfred North. *The Aims of Education and Other Essays* (first edition 1929), New American Library, New York, 1963.

Willingham, Warren W. *The Source Book for Higher Education,* College Entrance Examination Board, New York, 1973.

Woodring, Paul. *The Higher Learning in America: A Reassessment,* McGraw-Hill, New York, 1968.

Wolk, Ronald A. *Alternative Methods of Federal Funding for Higher Education,* Carnegie Commission on Higher Education, McGraw-Hill, New York, 1968.

1. The Implications of the Egalitarian Commitment

Anastasi, Anne, Martin J. Meade, and Alexander Schneiders. *The Validation of a Biographical Inventory as a Predictor of College Success,* Research Monograph No. 1, College Entrance Examination Board, New York, 1960.

Arrowsmith, William. "The Future of College Teaching," in *Campus 1980: The Shape of the Future in Higher Education,* Alvin Eurich, ed., Delacorte, New York, 1968.

Astin, Alexander W. *The College Dropout: A National Profile,* Research Report, American Council on Education, Vol. 7, No. 1, Washington, D.C., 1972.

———. "College Going and Human Development," *Change,* September 1962.

———. *The Educational and Vocational Development of Students,* American Council on Education, Washington, D.C., 1969.

———. "The Measured Effects of Higher Education," *Annals of the American Academy of Political and Social Science,* November, 1972.

———. *Predicting Academic Performance in College,* Free Press, New York, 1971.

————. "Undergraduate Achievement and Institutional 'Excellence'," *Science,* Vol. 161, August 1968.

————. *Who Goes Where to College,* Science Research Associates, Inc., Chicago, 1965.

Bayer, Alan E., David E. Drew, Alexander W. Astin, Robert F. Boruch, John A. Creager. *The First Year of College: A Follow-Up Normative Report,* Research Report, American Council on Education, Vol. 5, No. 1, Washington, D.C., 1970.

Belitsky, A. H. *Private Vocational Schools and Their Students: Unlimited Opportunities,* Schenkman Publishing Co., Cambridge, Mass., 1969.

Berls, Robert H. "An Exploration of the Determinants of Effectiveness in Higher Education," *The Economics and Financing of Higher Education,* A Compendium of Papers Submitted to the Joint Economic Committee, Congress of the United States, 91st Congress, 1st Session, U.S. Government Printing Office, Washington, D.C., 1969.

Birenbaum, William M. *Something for Everybody Is Not Enough. An Educator's Search for His Education,* Random House, New York, 1971.

Bok, Derek C. "The President's Report, 1971–72," *Harvard Today,* March 1973.

Bowles, Frank H. "The Evolution of Admissions Requirements," *College Admissions,* College Entrance Examination Board, Princeton, N.J., 1956.

Breneman, David W. *An Economic Theory of Ph.D. Production: The Case at Berkeley,* Office of the Vice-President, Planning and Analysis, University of California, Berkeley, 1970.

Burnham, Paul, and Albert Crawford. *Forecasting College Achievement,* Yale University Press, New Haven, 1946.

Carnegie Commission on Higher Education. *The Capitol and the Campus: State Responsibility and Higher Education,* McGraw-Hill, New York, 1971.

————. *A Chance to Learn. An Action Agenda for Equal Opportunity in Higher Education,* McGraw-Hill, New York, 1970.

————. *Continuities and Discontinuities: Higher Education and the Schools,* McGraw-Hill, New York, 1973.

————. *New Students and New Places: Policies for the Future Growth and Development of Higher Education,* McGraw-Hill, New York, 1971.

Change, February 1973.

Chickering, Arthur W. "The Best Colleges Have the Least Effect," *Saturday Review,* January 16, 1971.

Clark, Burton R. "The 'Cooling-Out' Function in Higher Education," *The American Journal of Sociology,* 1967.

Clark, Harold F., and Harold S. Sloan. *Classrooms on Mainstreet: An Account of Specialty Schools in the United States That Train for Work and Leisure,* Teachers College Press, Columbia University, New York, 1964.

Cobern, Morris, Claude Salem, and Selma Mushkin. *Indicators of Educational Outcome, Fall of 1972,* National Center for Educational Statistics, U.S. Government Printing Office, Washington, D.C., 1973.

Cohen, Arthur M., Florence B. Brawer, John Lombardi, John R. Boggs, Edgar A. Quimby, and Young Park. *A Constant Variable,* Jossey-Bass, San Francisco, 1971.

Coleman, James, et al. *Equality of Educational Opportunity,* U.S. Government Printing Office, Washington, D.C., 1966.

College and University Enrollment, Preliminary Survey, The University of the State of New York, The State Education Department, Albany, N.Y., 1969.

Cremin, Lawrence A. *The Transformation of the School,* Random House, New York, 1964.

Cross, K. Patricia. "The New Learners," *Change,* February 1973.

DeWitt, Laurence. "A Lottery System for Higher Education," *Notes on the Future of Education,* Educational Policy Center at Syracuse, Summer 1971.

Dressel, Paul L., and Irvin J. Lehmann. "The Impact of Higher Education on Student Attitudes, Values, and Critical Thinking Abilities," *Educational Record,* Summer 1966.

Eckaus, Richard S. *Estimating the Returns to Education,* Carnegie Commission on Higher Education, Berkeley, 1973.

Eurich, Alvin C., Lucien B. Kinney, and Sidney G. Tickton. *The Expansion of Graduate and Professional Education During the Period 1966 to 1980,* The Academy for Educational Development, Inc., New York, 1969.

Fitzgerald, Peter. *Democracy, Utility and Two Land Grant Colleges in the 19th Century: The Rhetoric and Reality of Reform,* dissertation submitted to Stanford School of Education, Stanford, California, July 1972.

Frankel, Charles. "The New Egalitarianism and the Old," *Commentary,* September 1973.

Froomkin, J. *Aspirations, Enrollments, and Resources,* U.S. Department of Health, Education, and Welfare, Office of Education, Washington, D.C., 1970.

Gardner, John. *Excellence,* Harper and Row, New York, 1961.

Goodman, Paul. *Compulsory Mis-Education,* Horizon Press, New York, 1964.

————. *Growing Up Absurd,* Random House, New York, 1960.

Gould, Samuel B., and K. Patricia Cross, eds. *Explorations in Non-Traditional Study,* Jossey-Bass, San Francisco, 1972.

Hansen, W. Less, and Burton A. Weisbrod. "The Search for Equity in the Provision and Finance of Higher Education," *The Economics and Financing of Higher Education in the United States,* A Compendium of Papers Submitted to the Joint Economic Committee, Congress of the United States, 91st Congress, 1st Session, U.S. Government Printing Office, Washington, D.C., 1969.

Hapgood, David. "Degrees: The Case for Abolition," *The Washington Monthly,* August 1969, pp. 6–13.

Hartman, Robert. "The Nixon Budget," *Change,* April 1973.

Harvard Educational Review, Vol. 38, No. 1, Winter 1968.

Healy, Timothy, Edward Quinn, Alexander Astin, and Jack Rossman. "The Case for Open Admissions," *Change,* Summer 1973, pp. 24–37.

Healy, Timothy S. "Will Everyman Destroy the University?" *Saturday Review,* December 20, 1969.

Heath, Douglas H. *Growing Up in College,* Jossey-Bass, San Francisco, 1968.

Heiss, Ann. *An Inventory of Academic Innovation and Reform,* Carnegie Commission on Higher Education, Berkeley, 1973.

Heist, Paul, ed. *The Creative College Student: An Unmet Challenge,* Jossey-Bass, San Francisco, 1968.

Hogan, Harry. "The BEOG Revolution," *Change,* Summer 1973.

Hodgkinson, Harold. "Goal-Setting and Evaluation," address to the National Foundation on New Planning and Management Practices in Higher Education," Denver, Colorado, Jan. 26, 1972.

————. "How Can We Measure the 'Value Added' to Students by College?" *Chronicle of Higher Education,* Nov. 13, 1972.

————. "Pass-Fail and the Protestant Ethic," *Chronicle of Higher Education,* Dec. 11, 1972.

Hoyt, Donald P. *The Relationship Between College Grades and Adult Achievement: A Review of the Literature,* ACT Research Report No. 7, American College Testing Service, Iowa City, Iowa, 1965.

Hudson, L. "Degree Class and Attainment in Scientific Research," *British Journal of Psychology,* Vol. 51, 1960.

Husén, Torsten. *Social Background and Educational Career: Research Perspectives on Equality of Educational Opportunity,* Centre for Educational Research and Innovation, Organization for Economic Cooperation and Development, Paris, 1972.

Illich, Ivan. *Deschooling Society,* Harrow Books, New York, 1970.

Jencks, Christopher, et al. *Inequality: A Reassessment of the Effects of Family and Schooling in America,* Basic Books, New York, 1972.

Karabel, Jerome. "Open Admissions: Toward Meritocracy or Democracy?" *Change,* May 1973.

Karabel, Jerome, and Alexander W. Astin. *Social Class, Academic Ability, and College "Quality,"* draft, American Council on Education, Washington, D.C., 1972.

"A Kind of Higher Education," *New York Times Magazine,* May 27, 1973.

Kohlberg, Lawrence, and Rochelle Mayer. "Development as the Aim of Education," *Harvard Educational Review,* Vol. 42, No. 4, November 1972.

Lawrence, Ben, George Weathersby, and Virginia W. Patterson, eds. *Outputs of Higher Education: Their Identification, Measurement and Evaluation,* Western Interstate Commission for Higher Education, Boulder, Colo., 1970.

Liberal Education. The Bulletin of the Association of American Colleges, Vol. 59, No. 1, March 1973.

Libow, Ken, and Ed Stuart. "Open Admissions: An Open and Shut Case?" *Saturday Review,* Dec. 9, 1972, p. 54.

Maclure, Stuart. "England's Open University," *Change,* March–April 1971.

Martin, Warren Bryan. *Conformity, Standards and Change in Higher Education,* Jossey-Bass, San Francisco, 1969.

Mayer, Martin. "Higher Education for All?" *Commentary,* Feb. 1973, pp. 37–47.

McClelland, David, ed. *The Achievement Motive,* Appleton-Century-Crofts, New York, 1953.

————. "Testing for Competence Rather Than Intelligence," *American Psychologist,* January 1973.

McGrath, Earl J., ed. *Prospect for Renewal,* Jossey-Bass, San Francisco, 1972.

————, ed. *Universal Higher Education,* McGraw-Hill, New York, 1966.

Medsker, Leland L., and James W. Trent. *Beyond High School: A Psychological Study of 10,000 High School Graduates*, Jossey-Bass, San Francisco, 1968.

Medsker, Leland L., and Dale Tillery. *Breaking the Access Barriers. A Profile of Two-Year Colleges*, McGraw-Hill, New York, 1971.

Milner, Murray. *The Illusion of Equality*, Jossey-Bass, San Francisco, 1972.

Moses, Stanley. *The Learning Force: A More Comprehensive Framework for Educational Policy*, Syracuse University, Syracuse, N.Y., 1971.

"The Open University," *Report on Education*, No. 56, Department of Education and Science, London, June 1969.

Opening Fall Enrollment in Higher Education, 1968, Summary Data, 1969; *Opening Fall Enrollment in Higher Education, 1969 —Basic Information: Report on Preliminary Survey*, 1971; *Advance Statistics on Opening Fall Enrollment in Higher Education, 1969: Basic Information*, 1970; *Advance Report on Opening Fall Enrollment in Higher Education, Institutional Data, 1970*, 1970; *Opening Fall Enrollment in Colleges and Universities, 1970, State and National Totals*, 1970. U.S. Department of Health, Education, and Welfare, Office of Education, Washington, D.C., 1970.

Perry, William G., Jr. *Forms of Intellectual and Ethical Development in College Years*, Holt, Rinehart and Winston, New York, 1970.

"Perspectives on *Inequality: A Reassessment of the Effect of Family and Schooling in America*," *Harvard Educational Review*, Vol. 43, No. 1, Winter 1973.

Project Talent, American Institutes for Research. *A National Data Resource for Behavioral Social and Educational Research*, Palo Alto, California, 1968.

"Question Marks on Marks," *New York Times*, Nov. 26, 1972.

Report of the Commission on Tests. Vol. I: *Righting the Balance;* Vol. II: *Briefs*, College Entrance Examination Board, Princeton, New Jersey, 1970.

Report on Higher Education: The Federal Role: Data and Decision-Making in Higher Education, Task Force Paper, Office of Education, Department of Health, Education, and Welfare, Washington, D.C., 1973.

Report on Higher Education: The Federal Role: Graduate Education, Task Force Paper, Office of Education, Department of Health, Education, and Welfare, Washington, D.C., March 1973.

Richards, James, Jr., John Holland, and Sandra Lutz. *The Prediction of Student Accomplishment in College,* ACT Research Report #13, June 1966.

Richards, James, Jr., and Sandra Lutz. *Predicting Student Success in College from the ACT Assessment,* ACT Research Report #21, August 1967.

Riesman, David. "Education at Harvard," *Change,* September 1973.

Rivlin, Alice. *The Federal Role in Higher Education,* The Brookings Institution, Washington, D.C., 1961.

Roose, Kenneth, and Charles Andersen. *A Rating of Graduate Programs,* American Council on Education, Washington, D.C., 1970.

Rossen, Joy, James Schoemer, and Patricia Nash. "Grades and Extra-Curricular Activities," *Journal of College Placement,* Feb.–Mar. 1973, pp. 73–76.

Sanford, Nevitt, ed. *The American College: A Psychological and Social Interpretation of the Higher Learning,* John Wilson & Sons, New York, 1962.

————. "New Values and Faculty Response," *Prospects for Renewal,* Earl J. McGrath, ed., Jossey-Bass, San Francisco, 1972.

————. *Where Colleges Fail,* Jossey-Bass, San Francisco, 1967.

Schraeder, W. B. "The Predictive Validity of College Board Admissions Tests," in *The College Board Admissions Testing Program,* William Angoff, ed., pp. 117–145, College Entrance Examination Board, New York, 1971.

Schudson, Michael S. "Organizing the 'Meritocracy': A History of the College Entrance Examination Board," *Harvard Educational Review*, Vol. 42, No. 1, February 1972.

Shell, Claude, and Floyd Patrick. "Grades Continue to Be Stressed by Recruiters," *Journal of College Placement*, Feb.–Mar. 1973, pp. 77–82.

Spaeth, Joe, and Andrew Greeley. *Recent Alumni and Higher Education*, McGraw-Hill, New York, 1970.

Taylor, C., W. R. Smith, and B. Ghiselin. "The Creative and Other Contributors of One Sample of Research Scientists," in *Scientific Creativity: Its Recognition and Development*, C. W. Taylor and F. Barron, eds., Wiley, New York, 1963.

Thorndike, R., and E. Hagen. *10,000 Careers*, Wiley, New York, 1959.

Thresher, B. Alden. *College Admissions and the Public Interest*, College Entrance Examination Board, New York, 1966.

Toward Equal Opportunity for Higher Education, College Entrance Examination Board, Princeton, N.J., 1973.

Trow, Martin. *Problems in the Transition from Elite to Mass Higher Education*, draft, prepared for 1973 OECD Conference on Mass Higher Education, Graduate School of Public Policy, University of California, Berkeley, June 1972.

Universal Higher Education: Costs and Benefits, Background Papers for participants in the 1971 Annual Meeting, American Council on Education, Washington, D.C.

Voeks, Virginia. *On Becoming an Educated Person: The University and College*, W. B. Saunders Company, Philadelphia, 1970.

Ward, F. Champion. "Liberal Arts Colleges and the Public Interest," paper prepared for conference on "A Policy for Education in the United States," at the Center for the Study of Democratic Institutions, March 19–20, 1963.

Willingham, Warren W. *Free-Access Higher Education*, College Entrance Examination Board, New York, 1970.

————. *The No. 2 Access Problem: Transfer to the Upper Division*, ERIC Research Report No. 4, American Association for Higher Education, Washington, D.C., 1972.

Wilms, Wellford W. "A New Look at Proprietary Schools," *Change,* Summer 1973.

Withey, Stephen B. *A Degree and What Else? Correlates and Consequences of a College Education,* Carnegie Commission on Higher Education, McGraw-Hill, New York, 1971.

Wolff, Robert Paul. *The Ideal of the University,* Beacon Press, Boston, 1969.

Wolfle, Dael. *America's Resources of Specialized Talent,* Report of the Commission of Human Resources and Advanced Training, Harper and Row, New York, 1954.

2. The End of Guaranteed Social Mobility

Adams, Walter, and A. J. Jaffe. "Economic Returns on the College Investment," *Change,* November 1971.

The American Freshman: National Norms for Fall 1971, American Council on Education, Office of Research, Washington, D.C., 1971.

American Indians, PC(2)-1F, Bureau of the Census, Washington, D.C., 1973.

Astin, Helen, Alexander W. Astin, Ann S. Bisconti, and Hyman H. Frankel. *Higher Education and the Disadvantaged Student,* Human Service Press, Washington, D.C., 1972.

Aurbach, Herbert A., Estelle Fuchs, and Gordon MacGregor. *The Status of the American Indian,* Pennsylvania State University, an Interim Report of the National Study of American Indian Education to the Office of Education, U.S. Department of Health, Education, and Welfare, Washington, D.C., 1970.

Backner, Burton L., and Lewis Bechenstein. "A Survey of Disadvantaged Students' Attitudes Towards a Special College Program," *The Journal of Human Resources,* Vol. 5, No. 1, 1970.

Baldridge, J. Victor, Jane Hannoway, Gary Riley, and George Ecker. *Equality of Opportunity in Higher Education and Its Impact on Career Mobility,* draft, Stanford University, Stanford, Calif., 1972.

Barnes, Sir Denis. "Technological Change and the Occupational Structure," International Conference on Automation, Full Employment and a Balanced Economy, Rome, 1967, The American Foundation on Automation and Employment, Inc.

Bayer, Alan E. *The Black College Freshman: Characteristics and Recent Trends,* American Council on Education Research Reports, Washington, D.C., 1972.

Bayer, Alan E., and Robert F. Boruch. "Black and White Freshmen Entering Four-Year Colleges," *Educational Record,* American Council on Education, Washington, D.C., Fall 1969.

Berls, Robert H. *Blacks and Higher Education,* draft, Brookings Institution, Washington, D.C., 1971.

The Black Student in American Colleges, ACE Research Reports, Vol. 4, No. 2, Office of Research, American Council on Education, Washington, D.C., 1969.

Blau, Peter, and Otis Duncan. *The American Occupational Structure,* Wiley & Sons, New York, 1967.

Bowen, Howard R., and Garth L. Mangum, *Automation and Economic Progress,* Prentice-Hall, Englewood Cliffs, N.J., 1966.

Bowles, Frank, and Frank A. DaCosta. *Between Two Worlds, A Profile of Historically Negro Colleges,* The Carnegie Commission on Higher Education, McGraw-Hill, New York, 1970.

Brimmer, Andrew F. "The Economic Outlook and the Future of the Negro College," *Daedalus,* Vol. 100, No. 3, Summer 1971.

Burn, Barbara. *Higher Education in Nine Countries,* Carnegie Commission on Higher Education, McGraw-Hill, New York, 1971.

Byrnes, James C. "On the Growth and Financing of Post-Secondary Education: Who Pays, Student or Taxpayer?" in *Post-Secondary Education: Where Do We Go from Here?,* Syracuse Educational Policy Research Center, Summer 1971.

Carnegie Commission on Higher Education. *A Chance to Learn: An Action Agenda for Equal Opportunity in Higher Education,* McGraw-Hill, New York, 1970.

———. *College Graduates and Jobs: Adjusting to a New Labor Market Situation,* McGraw-Hill, New York, 1973.

———. *From Isolation to Mainstream: Problems of the Colleges Founded for Negroes,* McGraw-Hill, New York, 1971.

Cartter, Allan M. *An Assessment of Quality in Graduate Education: A Comparative Study of Graduate Departments in 29 Academic Disciplines,* American Council on Education, Washington, D.C., 1966.

Characteristics of Successful Federally Supported "Special Services" Programs in Higher Education for Poverty and Minority Students, Educational Testing Service, Princeton, N.J., May 1973.

Coleman, James, et al. *Equality of Educational Opportunity,* U.S. Department of Health, Education, and Welfare, U.S. Government Printing Office, Washington, D.C., 1966.

College-Educated Workers, 1968–80: A Study of Supply and Demand, U.S. Department of Labor, Bureau of Labor Statistics, Bulletin No. 1676, 1970.

Colman, Joseph G., and Barbara A. Wheeler. *Human Uses of the University—Planning a Curriculum in Urban and Ethnic Affairs at Columbia University,* Praeger, New York, 1970.

Cross, K. Patricia. "The New Learners," *Change,* February 1973.

Crossland, Fred E. *Minority Access to College: A Ford Foundation Report,* Schocken Books, New York, 1971.

Dale, Arthur A. "Stability of Reasons for Going to College," *The Journal of Educational Research,* Vol. 63, No. 8, April 1970.

Dewey, John. *Experience and Education* (first edition 1938), Collier Books, New York, 1972.

DeWitt, Laurence B., and A. Dale Tussing. *The Supply and Demand for Graduates of Higher Education: 1970 to 1980,* Educational Policy Research Center, Syracuse University Research Corporation, Syracuse, N.Y., December 1971.

Earnings by Occupation and Education, 1970 Census of Population, U.S. Government Printing Office, Washington, D.C., 1973.

Eckaus, Richard. *Estimating the Returns to Education,* The Carnegie Commission on Higher Education, Berkeley, 1973.

Eckland, Bruce K. "Social Class and College Graduation: Some Misconceptions Corrected," *American Journal of Sociology,* 1964.

Egerton, John. *State Universities and Black Americans: An Inquiry into Desegregation and Equity for Negroes in 100 Public Universities,* Southern Education Reporting Service, May 1969.

Etzioni, Amitai, and Murray Milner. *Higher Education in an Active Society: A Policy Study,* Bureau of Social Science Research, Inc., Washington, D.C., March 1970.

Eysenck, H. J. "I.Q., Social Class and Educational Policy," *Change,* September 1973.

Farley, Reynolds. "The Quality of Demographic Data for Non-Whites," *Demography,* Vol. 5, No. 1, 1968.

Freeman, Richard B. *The Market for College-Trained Manpower: A Study in the Economics of Career Choice,* Harvard University Press, Cambridge, Mass., 1971.

Godwin, Winfred L., Thomas F. Pettigrew, St. Clair Drake, Andrew F. Brimmer, Tricia Roberts Harris, and Elias Blake, Jr. "The Future of the Black Colleges," *Daedalus,* Vol. 100, No. 3.

The Graduates: A Report on the Characteristics and Plans of College Seniors, Educational Testing Service, Princeton, N.J., 1973.

Green, Robert L. *The Admission of Minority Students: A Framework for Action,* Center for Urban Affairs, Michigan State University, East Lansing, Mich., 1970.

———. *Minority Group Students at Predominantly White Universities: Needs and Perspectives,* Center for Urban Affairs, Michigan State University, East Lansing, Mich., 1970.

Griggs vs. Duke Power Company, 91 S. Ct. 849 (March 8, 1971).

Hall, Wayne C. *The Graduate Marketplace: Current Status and Future Projections*, mimeo, National Research Council, 1970.

Harvard Educational Review, Vol. 38, No. 1, Winter 1968.

Heiss, Ann M. *Challenges to Graduate Schools*, Jossey-Bass, San Francisco, 1970.

Husén, Torsten. *Social Background and Education Career: Research Perspectives on Equality of Educational Opportunity*, Centre for Educational Research and Innovation, Organization for Economic Cooperation and Development, Paris, 1972.

Jaffe, A. J., and Walter Adams. *Academic and Socio-Economic Factors Related to Entrance and Retention at Two- and Four-Year Colleges in the Late 1960's*, Bureau of Applied Social Research, Columbia University, New York, 1970.

————. *1971–1972 Progress Report and Findings: Follow-Up of 1965–1966 High School Seniors and Related Higher Educational Materials*, Bureau of Applied Social Research, Columbia University, New York, 1971.

Jaffe, A. J., Walter Adams, and Sandro G. Meyers. *Negro Higher Education in the 60's*, Praeger, New York, 1968.

Jencks, Christopher, et al. *Inequality: A Reassessment of the Effect of Family and Schooling in America*, Basic Books, New York, 1972.

Jencks, Christopher, and David Riesman. "On Class in America," *The Public Interest*, Vol. 10, Winter 1968.

Johnstone, D. Bruce. *New Patterns for College Lending: Income Contingent Loans*, Columbia University Press, New York, 1972.

Karabel, Jerome, and Alexander W. Astin. *Social Class, Academic Ability, and College "Quality,"* draft, American Council on Education, Washington, D.C., 1972.

Katz, Joseph, Harold A. Korn, Carole A. Leland, and Max M. Levin. *Class, Character, and Career: Determinants of Occupational Choice in College Students*, Institute for the Study of Human Problems, Stanford University, Stanford, Calif., 1969.

Kilson, Martin. "The Black Experience at Harvard," *The New York Times Magazine,* Sept. 2, 1973.

Kitano, Harry H. L., and Dorothy L. Miller. *An Assessment of Education Opportunity Programs in California Higher Education,* Scientific Analysis Corporation, San Francisco, 1970.

Liebow, Elliot. *Tally's Corner,* Little, Brown & Co., Boston, 1966.

"Lifetime and Annual Income vs. Years of School Completed," *American Education,* Vol. 7, No. 33, March 1971.

Locke, Patricia. *Higher Education: Background and Implications for American Indians,* Western Interstate Commission on Higher Education, Boulder, Colo., 1973.

Manpower Report of the President, U.S. Department of Labor, U.S. Government Printing Office, 1972.

Mayhew, Lewis B. *Graduate and Professional Education, 1980: A Survey of Institutional Plans,* Carnegie Commission on Higher Education, McGraw-Hill, New York, 1970.

McCord, William, John Howard, Bernard Friedberg, and Edwin Harwood. *Life Styles in the Black Ghetto,* Norton, New York, 1969.

Medsker, Leland L., and James W. Trent. *Beyond High School: A Psychosocial Study of 10,000 High School Graduates,* Jossey-Bass, San Francisco, 1972.

Meyer, John W. *The Charter: Conditions of Diffuse Socialization in Schools,* Stanford University, Stanford, California, 1969.

Milner, Murray. *The Illusion of Equality: The Effects of Education on Opportunity, Inequality, and Social Conflict,* Jossey-Bass, San Francisco, 1972.

Mueller, Eva. *Technological Advance in an Expanding Economy,* Survey Research Center, Institute for Social Research, Ann Arbor, Michigan, 1969.

Nelson, Richard R., Merton J. Peck, and Edward D. Kalachec. *Technology, Economic Growth and Public Policy,* The Brookings Institution, Washington, D.C., 1967.

Nordheimer, Jon, " 'The Dream' 1973: Blacks Move Painfully Toward Full Equality," *New York Times,* Aug. 26, 1973.

"Perspectives on *Inequality: A Reassessment of the Effect of Family and Schooling in America,*" *Harvard Educational Review,* Vol. 43, No. 1, Winter 1973.

Project Talent, American Institutes for Research. *A National Data Resource for Behavioral Social and Educational Research,* Palo Alto, Calif., 1968.

Report of the Fall 1971 Undergraduate Ethnic Census of the City University of New York, CUNY, New York, 1972.

Riesman, David. "Education at Harvard," *Change,* September 1973.

Sanford, Nevitt. *Where Colleges Fail,* Jossey-Bass, San Francisco, 1967.

Sewell, William H., and Vimal P. Shah. "Socioeconomic Status, Intelligence, and the Attainment of Higher Education," *Sociology of Education,* Vol. 10, Winter 1970.

Silberman, Charles. *The Myths of Automation,* Harper and Row, New York, 1966.

Social and Economic Status of Negroes in the United States, Special Studies, Current Population Reports, Series 23, No. 38, Bureau of the Census, U.S. Department of Commerce, Washington, D.C., 1971.

Sowell, Thomas. *Black Education: Myths and Tragedies,* David McKay Co., New York, 1972.

Spaeth, Joe L., and Andrew M. Greeley. *Recent Alumni and Higher Education: A Survey of College Graduates,* Carnegie Commission on Higher Education, McGraw-Hill, New York, 1970.

Statistical Supplement to the Manpower Report of the President, 1965, U.S. Government Printing Office, Washington, D.C., 1965.

Toward Equal Opportunity for Higher Education, College Entrance Examination Board, Princeton, N.J., 1973.

Trow, Martin. *Problems in the Transition from Elite to Mass Higher Education,* draft, OECD Conference on Mass Higher Education, Graduate School of Public Policy, University of California, Berkeley, 1972.

Wattenburg, Ben J., and Richard M. Scammon. "Black Progress and Liberal Rhetoric," *Commentary,* April 1973 (response to that article, *Commentary,* August 1973).

Willie, Charles V., and Arline Sakuma McCord. *Black Students at White Colleges,* Praeger Special Studies in U.S. Economic and Social Development, New York, 1972.

Withey, Stephen B. *A Degree and What Else?,* Carnegie Commission on Higher Education, McGraw-Hill, New York, 1971.

Wolfle, Dael. *The Uses of Talent,* Princeton University Press, Princeton, N.J., 1971.

Work in America, Report of a Special Task Force to the Secretary of Health, Education, and Welfare, MIT Press, Cambridge, Mass., 1973.

3. New Requirements for Effective Education

Abert, James. "Money for Continuing Education," *Change,* October 1973.

"Admission and Retention of Students," Report of Master Plan Committee B, Illinois Board of Higher Education, June 1969.

Armstrong, Robert J., and Fred F. Harcleroad. *New Dimensions of Continuing Studies Programs in the Massachusetts State College System,* The American College Testing Program, Iowa City, Iowa, 1972.

Arrowsmith, William. "The Idea of a New University," *The Center Magazine,* March 1970.

The Aspen Notebook on the Cable and Continuing Education, papers from the Conference on the Cable and Continuing Education, Aspen, Colorado, June 1973.

Astin, Alexander W. *College Dropouts: A National Profile,* ACE Research Reports, Vol. 7, No. 1, American Council on Education, Washington, D.C., 1972.

————. *The Educational and Vocational Development of Students,* American Council on Education, Washington, D.C., 1969.

————. *Some New Directions for Higher Education: A Research Perspective,* American Council on Education, Washington, D.C., 1970.

————. "Undergraduate Achievement and Institutional 'Excellence,'" *Science,* Vol. 161, August 1968.

Astin, Alexander W., and Robert J. Panos. "Attrition Among College Students," *American Educational Research Journal,* Vol. 5, No. 1, January 1968.

Astin, Alexander W., Robert J. Panos, and John A. Creager. *National Norms for Entering College Freshmen, Fall 1966,* ACE Research Reports, Vol. 2, No. 1, Office of Research, American Council on Education, Washington, D.C., 1967.

Baskin, Samuel. "Universities: What 'Tearing Down the Wall' Can Do," *New York Times,* Education Section, Dec. 27, 1970.

Bayer, Alan E., David E. Drew, Alexander W. Astin, Robert F. Boruch, and John A. Creager. *The First Year of College: A Follow-Up Normative Report,* ACE Research Reports, Vol. 5, No. 1, Office of Research, American Council on Education, Washington, D.C., 1970.

Bell, Daniel. *The Reforming of General Education: The Columbia College Experience in Its National Setting,* Columbia University Press, New York, 1966.

Berelson, Bernard. *Graduate Education in the United States,* McGraw-Hill, New York, 1960.

Berg, Ivar. "Education and Performance: Some Problems," *Journal of Higher Education,* March 1972.

Berte, Neal R. *Innovations in Undergraduate Education: Selected Institutional Profiles and Thoughts about Experimentalism,* Report of the Conference, University of Alabama and National Science Foundation, Birmingham, Alabama, January 1972.

Birenbaum, William M. *Something for Everybody Is Not Enough: An Educator's Search for His Education,* Random House, New York, 1971.

Bok, Derek C. "The President's Report, 1971–72," *Harvard Today,* March 1973.

Bowen, Howard R., and Gordon K. Douglass. *Efficiency in Liberal Education: A Study of the Comparative Instructional Costs for Different Ways of Organizing Teaching-Learning in a Liberal Arts College,* Carnegie Commission on Higher Education, McGraw-Hill, New York, 1971.

Bowler, Mike. "Retraining Engineers into Urban Specialists," *Change,* Winter 1971–72.

Breedin, Brent. "Veterans in College," *Research Currents,* ERIC Clearinghouse in Higher Education, Washington, D.C., March 1972.

Brunner, Edmund, et al. *An Overview of Adult Education Research,* Adult Education Association of the U.S.A., Chicago, 1959.

Campbell, L. Howard, and Walter Hahn. "Readmission of Former Students after Absence from the Campus: Problems and Opportunities," *College and University,* Winter 1962.

Carnegie Commission on Higher Education. *The Campus and the City,* McGraw-Hill, New York, 1972.

———. *Continuities and Discontinuities: Higher Education and the Schools,* McGraw-Hill, New York, 1973.

———. *The Fourth Revolution: Instructional Technology in Higher Education,* McGraw-Hill, New York, 1972.

———. *Less Time, More Options: Education Beyond High School,* McGraw-Hill, New York, 1970.

———. *New Students and New Places: Policies for the Future Growth and Development of Higher Education,* McGraw-Hill, New York, 1971.

————. *The Open-Door Colleges: Policies for the Community Colleges,* McGraw-Hill, New York, 1970.

————. *Reform on Campus: Changing Students, Changing Academic Programs,* McGraw-Hill, New York, 1972.

Cartwright, Morse A. *Ten Years of Adult Education,* Macmillan Co., New York, 1935.

Change, February 1973.

"Characteristics of American Youth," *Technical Studies,* U.S. Department of Commerce, Bureau of the Census, Washington, D.C., 1970.

Clark, Burton R. "The 'Cooling-Out' Function in Higher Education," *The American Journal of Sociology,* 1967.

Clark, Harold F., and Harold S. Sloan. *Classrooms on Mainstreet: An Account of Specialty Schools in the United States that Train for Work and Leisure,* Teachers College Press, Columbia University, New York, 1964.

Colman, Joseph G., and Barbara A. Wheeler. *Human Uses of the University: Planning a Curriculum in Urban and Ethnic Affairs at Columbia University,* Praeger, New York, 1970.

Continuing Education Programs and Services for Women, U.S. Department of Labor, U.S. Government Printing Office, Washington, D.C., 1971.

Cope, Robert G. "Limitations of Attrition Rates and Causes Given for Dropping Out of College," *Journal of College Student Personnel,* Vol. 9, November 1968.

Cox, Charles E. "A Second Chance for Adults," *Change,* September 1973.

Cross, K. Patricia. *The Junior College Student: A Research Description,* Educational Testing Service, Princeton, N.J., 1968.

————. "The New Learners," *Change,* February 1973.

Dennis, Lawrence E., and Joseph F. Kauffman, eds. *The College and the Student,* American Council on Education, Washington, D.C., 1966.

Diversity by Design, Commission on Non-Traditional Study, Samuel B. Gould, Chairman, Jossey-Bass, San Francisco, 1973.

Douglas, Jack D. *Youth in Turmoil: America's Changing Youth Cultures and Student Protest Movements,* National Institute of Mental Health, Chevy Chase, Md., 1970.

Drew, David E., and John A. Creager. *The Vietnam-Era Veteran Enters College,* ACE Research Reports, Vol. 7, No. 4, 1972.

Eckland, Bruce K. "College Dropouts Who Came Back," *Harvard Educational Review,* 1964.

————. "A Source of Error in College Attrition Studies," *Sociology of Education,* Vol. 38, 1964.

Elsner, David M. "More Older Women Return to College; Most Do Very Well," *Wall Street Journal,* September 12, 1972.

Erikson, Erik. *Identity. Youth and Crisis,* Norton, New York, 1968.

Essert, Paul. *Creative Leadership of Adult Education,* Prentice-Hall, Englewood Cliffs, New Jersey, 1951.

Etzioni, Amitai, and Murray Milner. *Higher Education in an Active Society: A Policy Study,* Bureau of Social Science Research, Inc., Washington, D.C., 1970.

Eurich, Nell, and Barry Schwenkmeyer. *Great Britain's Open University: First Chance, Second Chance, or Last Chance?* Academy for Educational Development, New York, 1971.

Feldman, Kenneth A., ed. *College and Student: Selected Readings in the Social Psychology of Higher Education,* Pergamon Press, New York, 1972.

Fredericksen, Norman, and W. B. Schraeder. *Adjustment to College: A Study of 10,000 Veteran and Non-Veteran Students in Sixteen American Colleges,* Educational Testing Service, Princeton, N.J., 1951.

Furniss, W. Todd. *England's Open University: A Model for America?* Commission on Academic Affairs, May 1971.

Gibbons, James. *Employment of Educational Television,* draft, Stanford University, Stanford, California, 1969.

——. *New Structures for Higher Education Employing Educational Television,* Stanford University, Stanford, California, 1970.

Gideonse, Harry. "Educational Achievement of Veterans at Brooklyn College," *Educational Record,* October 1950.

Gould, Samuel B., and K. Patricia Cross, eds. *Explorations in Non-Traditional Study,* Jossey-Bass, San Francisco, 1972.

Graduate Education: Parameters for Public Policy, National Science Board, National Science Foundation, Washington, D.C., 1969.

Greeley, Andrew M. *From Backwater to Mainstream: A Profile of Catholic Higher Education,* Carnegie Commission on Higher Education, McGraw-Hill, New York, 1969.

Hall, Wayne C. *The Graduate Marketplace: Current Status and Future Projections,* mimeo, National Research Council, 1970.

Hechinger, Fred. "What 'Tearing Down the Walls' Can Do," *New York Times,* December 27, 1970.

Heiss, Ann. *Challenges to Graduate Schools,* Jossey-Bass, San Francisco, 1970.

——. *An Inventory of Academic Innovation and Reform,* Carnegie Commission on Higher Education, Berkeley, 1973.

Houle, Cyril O. *The Design of Education,* Jossey-Bass, San Francisco, 1972.

Houle, Cyril O., and John Summerskill. *The External Degree,* Jossey-Bass, San Francisco, 1972.

Hoyt, Donald P. *Forecasting Academic Success in Specific Colleges,* ACT Research Report No. 27, American College Testing Program, Iowa City, Iowa, 1968.

——. *The Relationship Between College Grades and Adult Achievement: A Review of the Literature,* ACT Research Report No. 7, American College Testing Program, Iowa City, Iowa, 1965.

Illich, Ivan. *Deschooling Society,* Harrow Books, New York, 1970.

―――. "Education Without School: How Can It Be Done?" Special Supplement, *The New York Review,* January 7, 1971.

Ingham, Roy J., ed. *Institutional Backgrounds of Adult Education: Dynamics of Change in the Modern University,* Center for the Study of Liberal Education for Adults at Boston University, Boston, 1966.

Jaffe, A. J., and Walter Adams. *Academic and Socio-Economic Factors Related to Entrance and Retention at Two- and Four-Year Colleges in the Late 1960's,* Bureau of Applied Social Research, Columbia University, New York, 1970.

―――. *American Higher Education in Transition,* Bureau of Applied Social Research, Columbia University, New York, 1969.

―――. *1971–1972 Progress Report and Findings: Follow-Up of 1965–1966 High School Seniors and Related Higher Educational Materials,* Bureau of Applied Social Research, Columbia University, New York, 1971.

Jones, Edward, and Gloria Ortner. *College Credit by Examination: An Evaluation of the University of Buffalo Program,* Univ. of Buffalo Studies, Vol. 21, No. 3, Univ. of Buffalo Press, Buffalo, N.Y., January 1954.

Kallen, Dennis. "European Views on Recurrent Education," *New Generation,* Fall 1972.

Katz, Joseph, et al. *No Time for Youth: Growth and Constraint in College Students,* Jossey-Bass, San Francisco, 1969.

Keniston, Kenneth. *The Uncommitted: Alienated Youth in American Society,* Harcourt, Brace & World, New York, 1965.

―――. "What's Bugging the Students," *Educational Record,* Vol. 51, No. 2, Spring 1970.

Knoell, Dorothy, and Leland Medsker. *Factors Affecting the Performance of Transfer Students from Two to Four Year Colleges,* U.S. Office of Education Cooperative Research Project No. 1133, University of California, Berkeley, 1964.

Knowles, Asa S., ed. *Handbook of College and University Administration,* McGraw-Hill, New York, 1970.

Knowles, Asa S., et al. *Handbook of Cooperative Education,* Jossey-Bass, San Francisco, 1971.

Knowles, Malcolm. *The Adult Education Movement in the United States,* Holt, Rinehart and Winston, New York, 1972.

Kreplin, Hannah. *Credit by Examination: A Review and Analysis of the Literature,* Research Program in University Administration, University of California, Berkeley, 1971.

Krumboltz, John D., and Carl E. Thoresen, eds. *Behavioral Counseling: Cases and Techniques,* Holt, Rinehart and Winston, New York, 1969.

Ladd, Dwight R. *Change in Educational Policy: Self-Studies in Selected Colleges and Universities,* Carnegie Commission on Higher Education, McGraw-Hill, New York, 1970.

Maclure, Stuart. "England's Open University," *Change,* March–April 1971.

Manpower Report to the President, U.S. Department of Labor, U.S. Government Printing Office, Washington, D.C., 1973.

Mansfield, Edwin. *The Economics of Technological Change,* Norton, New York, 1968.

Martin, Warren Bryan. *Alternative Forms of Higher Education for California,* Report to the Joint Committee on the Master Plan for Higher Education, California Legislature, Sacramento, 1973.

———. *Conformity: Standards and Change in Higher Education,* Jossey-Bass, San Francisco, 1969.

McClelland, David. "Testing for Competence Rather Than for 'Intelligence,' " *American Psychologist,* January 1973.

———, ed. *The Achievement Motive,* Appleton-Century-Crofts, New York, 1953.

McGrath, Earl J., ed. *Prospect for Renewal,* Jossey-Bass, San Francisco, 1972.

Medsker, Leland L., and James W. Trent. *Beyond High School: A Psychosocial Study of 10,000 High School Graduates,* Jossey-Bass, San Francisco, 1972.

Meyer, John W. *The Charter: Conditions of Diffuse Socialization in Schools,* Stanford University, Stanford, California, 1969.

Milton, Ohmer. *Alternatives to the Traditional,* Jossey-Bass, San Francisco, 1972.

Neighbor, J. Bruce. *Management Decisions in Lifelong Learning for the Next Decade: Developing and Utilizing New Channels to Opportunity,* draft, MCA, Inc., Universal City, Calif., 1970.

New Academic Institutions: A Survey, American Council on Education, Washington, D.C., 1972.

Olson, Keith. *A Historical Analysis of the G.I. Bill and Its Relationship to Higher Education,* U.S. Department of Health, Education, and Welfare, Office of Education, Bureau of Research, Washington, D.C., 1968.

"The Open-Door University," *Reports on Education,* No. 56, Department of Education and Science, London, June 1969.

Paraskevopoulos, John, and L. F. Robinson. "Comparison of College Performance of Cold War Veterans," *College and University,* Winter 1969.

Perl, Lewis J., and Martin R. Katzman. *Student Flows in California's System of Higher Education,* Office of the Vice-President for Planning and Analysis, University of California, Berkeley, 1969.

Perry, William G., Jr. *Forms of Intellectual and Ethical Development in the College Years,* Holt, Rinehart and Winston, New York, 1970.

Pervin, Lawrence A., Louis E. Reik, and Willard Dalrymple, eds. *The College Dropout and the Utilization of Talent,* Princeton University Press, Princeton, N.J., 1966.

Peterson, Richard E. "College Goals and the Challenge of Effectiveness," talk at Purdue University, Fort Wayne Campus, Nov. 23, 1971.

Piaget, Jean. *The Psychology of Intelligence,* Routledge and Kegan Paul, London, 1947.

Pifer, Alan. "Is It Time for an External Degree?" *College Board Review,* Winter 1970–71.

Project Talent, American Institutes for Research. *A National Data Resource for Behavioral Social and Educational Research,* Palo Alto, Calif., 1968.

"Recurrent Education: Constructing an Alternative," *New Generation,* Fall 1972.

Report of the American Bar Association, Commission on Campus Government and Student Dissent, American Bar Association, Chicago, 1969.

Report on Higher Education: The Federal Role: A GI Bill for Community Service, Task Force paper, Office of Education, Department of Health, Education, and Welfare, Washington, D.C., March 1973.

Report of the President's Commission on Campus Unrest (Scranton Commission), No. 277, Commerce Clearing House, Inc., Washington, D.C., 1970.

Richter, Melissa L., and Jan B. Whipple. *A Revolution in the Education of Women,* Sarah Lawrence College, Brownsville, N.Y., 1972.

Riesman, David, and Verne A. Stadtman, eds. *Academic Transformation: Seventeen Institutions Under Pressure,* Carnegie Commission on Higher Education, McGraw-Hill, New York, 1973.

Sanford, Nevitt. *Where Colleges Fail,* Jossey-Bass, San Francisco, 1967.

Schwebel, Milton. "Pluralism and Diversity in American Higher Education," *Annals of the American Academy of Political and Social Science,* November 1972.

Seivert, William A. "Senior Citizens Finding Open Doors at Many

Two-Year Colleges," *The Chronicle of Higher Education,* March 19, 1973.

Selected Problems in Innovation in American Higher Education, Study Performed for the Department of Health, Education, and Welfare, George Nolfi, Program Director, University Consultants, Inc., Cambridge, Mass., 1971.

Sharon, Amiel T. *College Credit for Off-Campus Study,* ERIC Clearinghouse on Higher Education, Washington, D.C., 1971.

Silberman, Charles E. *The Myths of Automation,* Harper & Row, New York, 1966.

Spurr, Stephen H. *Academic Degree Structures: Innovative Approaches: Principles of Reform in Degree Structures in the United States,* Carnegie Commission on Higher Education, McGraw-Hill, New York, 1970.

Stein, Gruno, and S. M. Miller. "Recurrent Education: An Alternative System," *New Generation,* Fall 1972.

Strassenburg, A. A. "External Degree Programs," *Journal of College Science Teaching,* Vol. 1, April 1972.

Striner, Herbert E. *Continuing Education as a National Capital Investment,* Upjohn Institute for Employment Research, Washington, D.C., 1971.

Summerskill, John. "Dropouts from College," in *The American College,* Nevitt Sanford, ed., Wiley, New York, 1962.

Super, Donald E., et al., *Computer-Assisted Counseling,* Teachers College Press, Columbia University, New York, 1970.

A Supplement to External Study for Post-Secondary Students: A Brief Annotated Bibliography of Recent Publications, Office of New Degree Programs, College Entrance Examination Board, Princeton, N.J., 1972.

A Survey of Returned Peace Corps Volunteers, Study #1929, Louis Harris and Associates, Inc., 1969.

To Improve Learning, A Report to the President and the Congress of the United States by the Commission on Instructional Technology, Committee on Education and Labor, House of Representatives, 91st Congress, 2d Session, Washington, D.C., 1970.

Towards New Structures of Post-Secondary Education, Organization for Economic Cooperation and Development, Paris, 1971.

Trow, Martin. "The Expansion and Transformation of Higher Education," to be published in *The International Review of Education,* UNESCO, Hamburg.

Tubbs, Walker E., ed. *Toward a Community of Seekers: A Report on Experimental Higher Education,* Johnston College National Symposium on Experimental Higher Education, January 1972.

The Undergraduate Student and His Higher Education: Withdrawal from College and Its Likelihood, Coordinating Council for Higher Education, Sacramento, 1969.

Universal Higher Education: Costs and Benefits, Background Papers for participants in the 1971 Annual Meeting, American Council on Education, Washington, D.C.

University of Toronto. *Career Information Services,* Career Counseling and Placement Centre, University of Toronto, Toronto, 1972.

University Without Walls: First Report, Union for Experimenting Colleges and Universities at Antioch College, Yellow Springs, Ohio, 1972.

Valentine, John. *The External Degree,* College Entrance Examination Board, New York, 1972.

Valley, John R. *Increasing the Options: Recent Developments in College and University Degree Programs,* Office of New Degree Programs, College Entrance Examination Board, Princeton, N.J., 1972.

Vermilye, Dyckman W., ed. *The Expanded Campus,* Jossey-Bass, San Francisco, 1972.

Ward, F. Champion. "Liberal Arts Colleges and the Public Interest," paper prepared for the Conference on a Policy for Education in the United States, Center for the Study of Democratic Institutions, Santa Barbara, Calif., March 19–20, 1963.

Wilms, Wellford W. "A New Look at Proprietary Schools," *Change,* Summer 1973.

Wolfle, Dael. *The Uses of Talent,* Princeton University Press, Princeton, N.J., 1971.

Work in America, Report of a Special Task Force to the Secretary of Health, Education, and Welfare, MIT Press, Cambridge, Mass., 1973.

4. New Political Realities

Abrahams, Louise. *State Planning for Higher Education,* The Academy for Educational Development, Inc., Washington, D.C., 1969.

Anderson, Paul, Ernest L. Boyer, and William McGill. "The Crisis of Money and Identity," *Change,* September 1972.

Ashworth, Kenneth H. *Scholars and Statesmen,* Jossey-Bass, San Francisco, 1972.

Astin, Alexander W. *Research-Based Decision Making in Higher Education: Possibility or Pipe Dream?,* draft, American Council on Education, Washington, D.C., 1973.

Bailey, Stephen K. "Combatting the Efficiency Cultists," *Change,* June 1973.

Balderston, F. E. *Financing Postsecondary Education. Statement to the Joint Committee on the Master Plan for Higher Education of the California Legislature,* Ford Foundation Program for Research in University Administration, University of California, Berkeley, 1972.

————. *Varieties of Financial Crisis,* Ford Foundation Program for Research in University Administration, University of California, Berkeley, 1972.

Baldridge, J. Victor. *Power and Conflict in the University,* John Wiley & Sons, New York, 1971.

Belitsky, A. H. *Private Vocational Schools and Their Students: Unlimited Opportunities,* Schenkman Publishing Co., Cambridge, Mass., 1969.

Benet, James. "California's Regents: Window on the Ruling Class," *Change,* February 1972.

Bennis, Warren, and Patricia Ward Biederman. *The Leaning Ivory Tower,* Jossey-Bass, San Francisco, 1973.

Berdahl, Robert O. *Statewide Coordination of Higher Education,* American Council on Education, Washington, D.C., 1971.

Berg, Ivar E. "Rich Man's Qualifications for Poor Man's Jobs," *Trans-Action,* March 1969.

Bolton, Roger E. "The Economics and Public Financing of Higher Education: An Overview," in *The Economics and Financing of Higher Education,* A Compendium of Papers Submitted to the Joint Economic Committee of the U.S. Congress, 91st Congress, 1st Session, U.S. Government Printing Office, Washington, D.C., 1969.

Bowen, Howard R. "Does Private Education Have a Future?" speech delivered in Cincinnati, Ohio, at the annual meeting of the Association of American Colleges, January 12, 1971.

————. *The Finance of Higher Education,* Carnegie Commission on Higher Education, McGraw-Hill, New York, 1968.

————. "Tuitions and Student Loans in the Finance of Higher Education," in *The Economics and Financing of Higher Education,* A Compendium of Papers Submitted to the Joint Economic Committee of the U.S. Congress, 91st Congress, 1st Session, U.S. Government Printing Office, Washington, D.C., 1969.

Bowen, Howard R., and Paul Servelle. *Who Benefits from Higher Education—and Who Should Pay?,* American Association for Higher Education, Washington, D.C., 1972.

Boyd, William. "Collective Bargaining in Academe: Causes and Consequences," *Liberal Education,* October 1971.

Bunzel, John H. "The Politics of Quotas," *Change,* October 1972.

Carnegie Commission on Higher Education. *The Campus and the City,* McGraw-Hill, New York, 1972.

――――. *The Capitol and the Campus,* McGraw-Hill, New York, 1971.

――――. *Governance of Higher Education,* McGraw-Hill, New York, 1973.

――――. *Institutional Aid,* McGraw-Hill, New York, 1972.

――――. *The Open-Door Colleges: Policies for the Community Colleges,* McGraw-Hill, New York, 1970.

Carr, Robert A., and Daniel K. Vaneyck. *Collective Bargaining Comes to the Campus,* American Council on Education, Washington, D.C., 1973.

Cheit, Earl F. *The New Depression in Higher Education: A Study of Financial Conditions at 41 Colleges and Universities,* Carnegie Commission on Higher Education, McGraw-Hill, New York, 1970.

――――. *The New Depression in Higher Education—Two Years Later,* Carnegie Commission on Higher Education, Berkeley, 1973.

Cohen, Audrey. *New Tests to Measure Job Skills and Determine Effective Performance,* College for Human Services, New York, 1970.

Collective Bargaining on Campus, ERIC Clearinghouse on Higher Education, American Association for Higher Education, Washington, D.C., 1972.

College-Educated Workers, 1968–80: A Study of Supply and Demand, U.S. Department of Labor, Bureau of Labor Statistics, Bulletin no. 1676, 1970.

Contemporary Educational Issues, George Washington University, Viewpoints, Institute for Educational Leadership, Washington, D.C., 1972.

Continuing Education Programs and Services for Women, U.S. Department of Labor, U.S. Government Printing Office, Washington, D.C., 1971.

Cosand, Joseph. "The Community College in 1980," in *Campus 1980: The Shape of the Future in Higher Education,* ed. Alvin Eurich, Delacorte, New York, 1968.

Doherty, Robert. "The National Labor Relations Act and Higher Education," *National Association of College and University Officers Professional File,* June 1973.

Dressel, Paul L., and William H. Faricy. *Return to Responsibility,* Jossey-Bass, San Francisco, 1972.

Dunham, E. Alden, and David Riesman. *Colleges of the Forgotten Americans,* McGraw-Hill, New York, 1969.

Education Directory: Higher Education, 1972–1973, National Center for Educational Statistics, Office of Education, Department of Health, Education, and Welfare, Washington, D.C., 1972.

Edwards, Scott. "An Academic Chairman Looks at Governance," *Change,* September 1972.

Eulau, Heinz, and Harold Quinley. *State Officials and Higher Education: A Survey of the Opinions and Expectations of Policy Makers in Nine States,* Carnegie Commission on Higher Education, McGraw-Hill, New York, 1970.

Faculty Tenure, Report of the Commission on Academic Tenure in Higher Education, Jossey-Bass, San Francisco, 1973.

Glenny, Lyman A. *The Anonymous Leaders of Higher Education,* Center for Research and Development in Higher Education, University of California, Berkeley, 1971.

Glenny, Lyman A., Robert O. Berdahl, Ernest G. Palola, and James G. Baldridge. *Coordinating Higher Education for the '70's,* Center for Research and Development in Higher Education, University of California, Berkeley, 1971.

Godwin, Winfred L., and Peter B. Mann. *Higher Education: Myths, Realities, and Possibilities,* Southern Regional Education Board, Atlanta, Georgia, 1972.

The Governing of Princeton University: Final Report of the Special Committee on the Structure of the University, Princeton University, Princeton, N.J., 1970.

Hapgood, David. "Degrees: The Case for Abolition," *The Washington Monthly,* August 1969.

Hechinger, Fred. "Is Common Action Possible?" *Change,* September 1972.

Hodgkinson, Harold L. *Campus Governance: The Amazing Thing Is That It Works at All,* ERIC Clearinghouse on Higher Education, Washington, D.C., 1971.

Hoyt, David P. *The Relationship Between College Grades and Adult Achievement: A Review of the Literature,* Research Report No. 7, American College Testing Service, Iowa City, Iowa, Fall, 1965.

Kerr, Clark. *The Uses of the University,* Harper Torchbooks, New York, 1963.

Knowles, Asa S., et al. *Handbook of Cooperative Education,* Jossey-Bass, San Francisco, 1971.

Lee, Eugene C., and Frank M. Bowen. *The Multicampus University. A Study of Academic Governance,* The Carnegie Commission on Higher Education, McGraw-Hill, New York, 1971.

Levin, Henry M. "Vouchers and Social Equity," *Change,* Sept. 1972.

Livingston, Sterling. "Myth of the Well Educated Manager," *Harvard Business Review,* January–February, 1971.

Master Plan for Higher Education in California, 1960–1975, Legislature of the State of California, 1960, in cooperation with the State Department of Education; implemented in the Donahoe Act, 1960, Sacramento.

A Master Plan for Higher Education in Illinois—Phase III, Illinois Board on Higher Education, Springfield, Illinois, 1971.

Maynard, James. *Some Microeconomics of Higher Education,* University of Nebraska Press, Lincoln, Nebraska, 1971.

Miller, S. M. "Alternatives to Schools," *New York University Education Quarterly,* Vol. 1, No. 4, Summer 1970.

———. "Strategies for Reducing Credentialism," *ACTION,* Summer 1970.

More Scholars Per Dollar, Public Policy Research Organization, University of California, Irvine, 1971.

Mortimer, Kenneth P. *Accountability in Higher Education,* American Association for Higher Education, Washington, D.C., 1972.

New Dimensions of Continuing Studies Programs in the Massachusetts State College System, American College Testing Program, Iowa City, Iowa, 1972.

O'Neil, Robert M. *The Courts, Government and Higher Education,* Committee for Economic Development, New York, 1972.

O'Neill, June A. *Sources of Funds to Colleges and Universities,* Carnegie Commission on Higher Education, Berkeley, 1973.

The Outputs of Higher Education: Their Identification, Measurement, and Evaluation, Western Interstate Commission for Higher Education, Denver, 1970.

Palola, Ernest, T. Lenman, and W. R. Blischke. *Higher Education by Design: The Sociology of Planning,* Center for Research and Development in Higher Education, University of California, Berkeley, 1969.

Papers and Proceedings of the Conference on Recurrent Education, Organization for Economic Cooperation and Development, held at Georgetown University, Washington, D.C., March 1973.

Park, Dabney, Jr. "A Loyal AAUP Member Says: 'Down With Tenure,'" *Change,* March 1972.

Pottinger, J. Stanley. "The Drive Toward Equality," *Change,* October 1972.

Progress Report, 1965–69, Center for Research and Development in Higher Education, University of California, Berkeley, 1969.

"Report of the Committee on Private Universities and Private Giving," *The University of Chicago Record,* April 21, 1973.

Report of the Joint Committee on the Master Plan for Higher Education, California Legislature, Sacramento, 1973.

Report on Licensure and Related Health Personnel Credentialing, U.S. Department of Health, Education, and Welfare, Washington, D.C., June 1971.

Report of the President's Commission on Campus Unrest, ARNO Press, New York, 1970.

Riesman, David, and Verne A. Stadtman, eds. *Academic Transformation. Seventeen Institutions Under Pressure,* Carnegie Commission on Higher Education, McGraw-Hill, New York, 1973.

Rivlin, Alice M., and June O'Neill. "Growth and Change in Higher Education," in *The Corporation and the Campus: Corporate Support of Higher Education in the 1970's,* Robert H. Connery, ed., The Academy of Political Science, Columbia University, New York, 1970.

Shulman, Carol H. *Affirmative Action: Women's Rights on Campus,* American Association for Higher Education, Washington, D.C., 1972.

———. *Collective Bargaining on Campus,* American Association for Higher Education, Washington, D.C., 1972.

———. *State Aid to Private Higher Education,* American Association for Higher Education, Washington, D.C., 1972.

Smith, G. Kerry, ed. *Agony and Promise,* Jossey-Bass, San Francisco, 1969.

Spurr, Stephen H. *Academic Degree Structures: Innovative Approaches: Principles of Reform in Degree Structures in the United States,* Carnegie Commission on Higher Education, McGraw-Hill, New York, 1970.

State Aid to Private Higher Education, A Study of Ways of Providing Public Resources for Support of Private Institutions of Higher Education in California, ERIC Clearinghouse on Higher

Education, American Association for Higher Education, Washington, D.C., 1972.

Statewide Planning for Postsecondary Education, Western Interstate Conference on Higher Education, Boulder, Colorado, 1971.

Striner, Herbert. *Continuing Education as a National Capital Investment,* Upjohn Institute for Employment Research, Washington, D.C., 1971.

Summary of State Legislation Affecting Higher Education in the West, 1969, Western Interstate Commission for Higher Education, Boulder, Colorado, 1969.

Thomson, Francis C., ed. *The New York Times Guide to Continuing Education in America,* Quadrangle Books, New York, 1972.

Tollett, Kenneth S. "The Faculty and the Government," speech to the 56th Annual Meeting of the American Council on Education, Washington, D.C., October 1973.

Tolo, Kenneth W., ed. *Educating a Nation: The Changing American Commitment,* Lyndon B. Johnson School of Public Affairs, University of Texas at Austin, Austin, 1973.

Toombs, William. *Productivity: Burden of Success,* American Association for Higher Education, Washington, D.C., 1973.

Tyler, Gus. "The Faculty Joins the Proletariat," *Change,* Winter 1971–72.

Vermilye, Dyckman W., ed. *The Expanded Campus,* Jossey-Bass, San Francisco, 1972.

Wollett, Donald. "The Status and Trend of Collective Negotiations for Faculty in Higher Education," *Wisconsin Law Review,* 1971.

5. The Federal Presence in Higher Education

Ashworth, Kenneth H. *Scholars and Statesmen,* Jossey-Bass, San Francisco, 1972.

Bowen, Howard R. *The Finance of Higher Education,* Carnegie Commission on Higher Education, McGraw-Hill, New York, 1968.

Bush, Vannevar. *Science, the Endless Frontier,* Report to the President on a Program for Post-War Scientific Research, U.S. Government Printing Office, Washington, D.C., 1945.

Carnegie Commission on Higher Education. *The Capitol and the Campus: State Responsibility for Higher Education,* McGraw-Hill, New York, 1971.

————. *Institutional Aid—Federal Support to Colleges and Universities,* McGraw-Hill, New York, 1972.

————. *Quality and Equality: New Levels of Federal Responsibility for Higher Education,* McGraw-Hill, New York, 1968.

————. *Quality and Equality: Revised Recommendations on New Levels of Federal Responsibility for Higher Education,* McGraw-Hill, New York, 1970.

Cheit, Earl F. *The New Depression in Higher Education—Two Years Later,* Carnegie Commission on Higher Education, McGraw-Hill, New York, 1973.

Dupree, A. Hunter. *Science in the Federal Government,* Harvard University Press, Cambridge, Mass., 1957.

Dupree, J. Stefan, and Sanford A. Lakoff. *Science and the Nation,* Prentice-Hall, Englewood Cliffs, N.J., 1962.

Federal Funds for Academic Science: Fiscal Year 1969, National Science Foundation, Washington, D.C., 1971.

The Federal Government and Higher Education, American Assembly, Columbia University, Prentice-Hall, Englewood Cliffs, N.J., 1960.

Federal Support for Academic Science and Other Educational Activities in Universities and Colleges: Fiscal Years 1963–66, National Science Foundation, Washington, D.C., 1967.

Federal Support to Universities and Colleges: Fiscal Year 1967, National Science Foundation, U.S. Government Printing Office, Washington, D.C., 1968.

Federal Support to Universities, Colleges and Selected Non-Profit Institutions, Fiscal Year 1971, National Science Foundation, NSF 73-300, U.S. Government Printing Office, Washington, D.C., 1973.

Fields, Cheryl M. "U.S. Involvement in State Planning Alarms Colleges," *Chronicle of Higher Education,* Dec. 18, 1972.

Fitzgerald, Peter. *Democracy, Utility and Two Land-Grant Colleges in the Nineteenth Century: The Rhetoric and the Reality of Reform,* dissertation, Stanford University, 1972.

Froomkin, Joseph. *Students and Buildings: An Analysis of Selected Federal Programs for Higher Education,* Office of Education, Department of Health, Education, and Welfare, U.S. Government Printing Office, Washington, D.C., 1968.

Handbook on Programs of the U.S. Department of Health, Education, and Welfare, U.S. Government Printing Office, Washington, D.C., 1965.

Hartman, Robert W. *The Rationale for Federal Support of Higher Education,* draft, U.S. Office of Education, 1972.

Hogan, Harry J. *Higher Education: The Relationship Between Money and Mission,* draft, Washington, D.C., 1972.

Kerr, Clark. "Federal Aid to Higher Education Through 1976," in *The Economics and Financing of Higher Education,* A Compendium of Papers Submitted to the Joint Economic Committee of the U.S. Congress, 91st Congress, 1st Session, U.S. Government Printing Office, Washington, D.C., 1969.

Kidd, Charles V. *American Universities and Federal Research,* Belknap Press, Cambridge, Mass., 1959.

Miller, J. H., and John S. Allen. *Veterans Challenge the Colleges: The New York Program,* King's Crown Press, Columbia University, New York, 1947.

National Patterns of Research and Development Resources: Funds and Manpower in the United States, 1953–70, National Science Foundation, U.S. Government Printing Office, Washington, D.C., 1969.

National Patterns of Research and Development Resources: Funds and Manpower in the United States, 1953–71, National Science Foundation, NSF 70-46, U.S. Government Printing Office, Washington, D.C., 1972.

Olson, Keith. *A Historical Analysis of the G.I. Bill and its Relationship to Higher Education,* Department of Health, Education, and Welfare, Office of Education, Bureau of Research, Washington, D.C., 1968.

O'Neill, June A. *Sources of Funds to Colleges and Universities,* Carnegie Commission on Higher Education, Berkeley, 1973.

Orlans, Harold. *The Effects of Federal Programs on Higher Education,* The Brookings Institution, Washington, D.C., 1962.

Orwig, M. D., ed. *Financing Higher Education: Alternatives for the Federal Government,* American College Testing Program, Iowa City, Iowa, 1971.

Quattlebaum, Charles A. *Federal Educational Policies, Programs and Proposals: A Survey and Handbook,* 3 parts, U.S. Government Printing Office, Washington, D.C., 1960.

Report on Federal Postdoctoral Support, Part 1, Fellowships and Traineeships, Federal Interagency Committee on Education, Washington, D.C., April 1970.

Richardson, Elliot L. *Responsibility and Responsiveness (II): A Report on the HEW Potential for the Seventies,* Department of Health, Education, and Welfare, Washington, D.C., 1973.

Rivlin, Alice M. *The Role of the Federal Government in Financing Higher Education,* The Brookings Institution, Washington, D.C., 1961.

Schultze, Charles L., Edward R. Fried, Alice M. Rivlin, and Nancy H. Teeters. *Setting National Priorities. The 1972 Budget,* The Brookings Institution, Washington, D.C., 1971.

Schultze, Charles L., Edward K. Hamilton, and Allen Schick. *Setting National Priorities. The 1971 Budget,* The Brookings Institution, Washington, D.C., 1970.

Social Welfare Expenditures Under Public Programs in the United States 1929–1966, U.S. Department of Health, Education, and Welfare, Social Security Administration, Office of Research and Statistics, Report No. 25, Washington, D.C., 1968.

Tax Reform and the Crisis of Financing Higher Education, Report of the Association of American Universities, Washington, D.C., May 1973.

Tolo, Kenneth W., ed. *Educating a Nation: The Changing American Commitment,* Lyndon B. Johnson School of Public Affairs, University of Texas at Austin, Austin, 1973.

Toward a Long-Range Plan for Federal Financial Support for Higher Education, U.S. Department of Health, Education, and Welfare, Washington, D.C., 1969.

United States Government Organization Manual, 1972–73, Office of the Federal Register, National Archives and Records Service, GSA, U.S. Government Printing Office, Washington, D.C., 1973.

Van Alstyne, Carol. *Sources of Support for Higher Education: Historical Trends,* American Council on Education, Washington, D.C., 1973.

Whealen, John J. *A History of Federal Aid to Education, 1785– 1965,* ERIC Research in Education, document no. ED 033-161, Washington, D.C., 1965.

6. The Federal Role in Postsecondary Education

Astin, Alexander, and Robert C. Nichols. "Progress of the Merit Scholar: An Eight Year Follow-Up," *Personnel and Guidance Journal,* March 1966.

Balderston, F. E. *Financing Postsecondary Education. Statement to the Joint Committee on the Master Plan for Higher Education of the California Legislature,* Ford Foundation Program for Research in University Administration, University of California, Berkeley, 1972.

Baldridge, J. Victor. *Power and Conflict in the University,* John Wiley & Sons, New York, 1971.

Bowen, Howard R. "Tuitions and Student Loans in the Finance of Higher Education," in *The Economics and Financing of Higher Education in the United States,* A Compendium of Papers

Submitted to the Joint Economic Committee, Congress of the United States, 91st Congress, 1st Session, U.S. Government Printing Office, Washington, D.C., 1969.

————. *The Finance of Higher Education,* Carnegie Commission on Higher Education, McGraw-Hill, New York, 1968.

Bowen, William G. *The Economics of the Major Private Universities,* Carnegie Commission on Higher Education, McGraw-Hill, New York, 1968.

Carnegie Commission on Higher Education. *Quality and Equality: New Levels of Federal Responsibility for Higher Education,* McGraw-Hill, New York, 1968.

Center for the Study of Public Policy. *Education Vouchers. A Report on Financing Elementary Education by Grants to Parents,* Center for the Study of Public Policy, Cambridge, Mass., 1970.

Daniere, Andre. "The Benefits and Costs of Alternative Federal Programs of Financial Aid to College Students," in *The Economics and Financing of Higher Education in the United States,* A Compendium of Reports Submitted to the Joint Economic Committee, Congress of the United States, 91st Congress, 1st Session, U.S. Government Printing Office, Washington, D.C., 1969.

Eckaus, Richard S. *Estimating the Returns to Education,* Carnegie Commission on Higher Education, Berkeley, 1973.

Expanding Opportunities: Case Studies of Interinstitutional Cooperation, Southern Regional Education Board, Atlanta, Georgia, 1969.

Faculty Participation in Academic Governance, American Association of Higher Education, Washington, D.C., 1967.

Federal Agencies and Black Colleges—Fiscal 1970, Federal Inter-Agency Committee on Education, Washington, D.C., 1972.

Federal Support to Universities and Colleges. Fiscal Year 1967, National Science Foundation, U.S. Government Printing Office, Washington, D.C., 1968.

Finn, Chester E., Jr. "The National Foundation for Higher Education: Death of an Idea," *Change,* March 1972.

Five College Cooperation: Directions for the Future, University of Massachusetts Press, Amherst, Mass., 1969.

Freedman, Richard. *The Market for College-Trained Manpower: A Study in the Economics of Career Choice,* Harvard University Press, Cambridge, Mass., 1971.

Froomkin, J. *Aspirations, Enrollments, and Resources,* U.S. Department of Health, Education, and Welfare, Office of Education, Washington, D.C., 1970.

Godwin, Winfred L. "Interinstitutional and Interstate Cooperation in American Higher Education," paper presented to the College of Europe symposium *Towards a European Policy of Higher Education: Goals and Methods,* Brussels, Belgium, April 1973.

Goodfriend, Harvey J. "The University as Public Utility," *Change,* March 1973.

Hansen, W. Lee, and Burton A. Weisbrod. "The Search for Equity in the Provision and Finance of Higher Education," in *The Economics and Financing of Higher Education in the United States,* A Compendium of Papers Submitted to the Joint Economic Committee, Congress of the United States, 91st Congress, 1st Session, U.S. Government Printing Office, Washington, D.C., 1969.

Hartman, Robert W. *The Rationale for Federal Support for Higher Education,* draft, U.S. Office of Education, Washington, D.C., 1972.

Heiss, Ann. *An Inventory of Academic Innovation and Reform,* Carnegie Commission on Higher Education, Berkeley, 1973.

It Works Series: Summaries of Selected Compensatory Education Projects, U.S. Office of Education, U.S. Government Printing Office, Washington, D.C., 1970.

Maynard, James. *Some Microeconomics of Higher Education— Economies of Scale,* University of Nebraska Press, Lincoln, Nebraska, 1971.

Millett, John. *Decisionmaking and Administration in Higher Education,* Kent State University Press, Kent, Ohio, 1968.

More Scholars Per Dollar, 2d Printing, Public Policy Research Organization, University of California at Irvine, Irvine, California, 1971.

Mortimer, Kenneth. *Accountability in Higher Education,* ERIC Clearinghouse on Higher Education, American Association for Higher Education, Washington, D.C., 1972.

O'Neil, Robert M. *The Courts, Government and Higher Education,* Committee for Economic Development, New York, 1972.

Orwig, M. D., ed. *Financing Higher Education: Alternatives for the Federal Government,* American College Testing Program, 1971.

Quattlebaum, Charles A. *Federal Education Policies, Programs and Proposals: A Survey and Handbook,* 3 parts, U.S. Government Printing Office, Washington, D.C., 1960.

Riesman, David, and Verne A. Stadtman, eds. *Academic Transformation. Seventeen Institutions Under Pressure,* Carnegie Commission on Higher Education, McGraw-Hill, New York, 1973.

Rivlin, Alice. *The Role of the Federal Government in Financing Higher Education,* The Brookings Institution, Washington, D.C., 1971.

Rivlin, Alice M., and Jeffrey H. Weiss. "Social Goals and Federal Support of Higher Education—The Implications of Various Strategies," in *Economics and Financing of Higher Education in the United States,* A Compendium of Papers Submitted to the Joint Economic Committee, Congress of the United States, 91st Congress, 1st Session, U.S. Government Printing Office, Washington, D.C., 1969.

Schultz, Theodore W. "Resources for Higher Education: An Economist's View," *The Journal of Political Economy,* Vol. 76, No. 3, May/June 1968.

Segal, David. " 'Equity' Versus 'Efficiency' in Higher Education," in *Economics and Financing of Higher Education in the United*

States, A Compendium of Papers Submitted to the Joint Economic Committee, Congress of the United States, 91st Congress, 1st Session, U.S. Government Printing Office, Washington, D.C., 1969.

Simon, Kenneth A. "The Planning of U.S. Higher Education: Projections of Enrollment, Degrees, Staff, and Expenditures to 1977–78," in *Economics and Financing of Higher Education in the United States,* A Compendium of Papers Submitted to the Joint Economic Committee, Congress of the United States, 91st Congress, 1st Session, U.S. Government Printing Office, Washington, D.C., 1969.

Singer, Neil, and Paul Feldman. "Criteria for Public Investment in Higher Education," in *Economics and Financing of Higher Education in the United States,* A Compendium of Papers Submitted to the Joint Economic Committee, Congress of the United States, 91st Congress, 1st Session, U.S. Government Printing Office, Washington, D.C., 1969.

Statewide Planning for Postsecondary Education, Western Interstate Commission for Higher Education, Boulder, Colo., 1971.

Tolo, Kenneth W., ed. *Educating a Nation: The Changing American Commitment,* Lyndon B. Johnson School of Public Affairs, University of Texas at Austin, Austin, 1973.

Toombs, William. *Productivity: Burden of Success,* ERIC Higher Education Research Report No. 2, American Association for Higher Education, Washington, D.C., 1973.

Van Alstyne, Carol. *Sources of Support for Higher Education: Historical Trends,* American Council on Education, Washington, D.C., 1973.

Wentworth, Eric. "The Higher Education Act—and Beyond," *Change,* September 1972.